Federico García Lorca

Poems of Love & Death

Translated into English by
A. S. Kline

Poetry In Translation
www.poetryintranslation.com

© 2007-2023 A. S. Kline

Cover design by Poetry in Translation

Digital scans or photographs of the images in the main text have been released into the public domain by various institutions. Identifications and attributions are provided beneath each image. All related image rights are at the discretion of the copyright holders of the original images and/or the referenced institutions.

All rights reserved under International and Pan American Copyright Conventions. Textual content of this work may be freely reproduced, stored and transmitted, electronically or otherwise, for any non-commercial purpose. Restrictions apply to adaptation of the work. Usage of any material for commercial purposes resulting in direct, indirect or incidental commercial gain requires permission to be sought and granted in writing from the copyright holder. Refer to the Poetry in Translation copyright statement (*www.poetryintranslation.com/Admin/Copyright.php*)

Any statements or opinions expressed in this book reflect the views of the author alone. Although the author has made every effort to ensure that the information in this book was correct at the time of going to press, the author does not assume and hereby disclaims any liability to any party for any loss, damage, or disruption caused by errors or omissions, whether such errors or omissions result from negligence, accident, or any other cause

Please direct sales or editorial enquiries to:
tonykline@poetryintranslation.com

This print edition is published by
Poetry In Translation (*www.poetryintranslation.com*),
via Amazon EU S.à.r.l. (a Luxembourg company with registration number B-101818 and its registered office at 5 Rue Plaetis, L-2338, Luxembourg)

ISBN-13: 979-8-3865-7701-8

❝ *Y mi sangre sobre el campo
sea rosado y dulce limo
donde claven sus azadas
los cansados campesinos.* ❞

(*From: Cicada! – Libro de Poemas, 1921*)

Contents

Translator's Introduction 8

From: Libro de Poemas, 1921 9
Weather-Vane (Veleta) 9
New Songs (Cantos Nuevos) 12
Dream (Sueño) 14
Ballad of the Small Plaza (Balada de la placate) 16
The Ballad of the Salt-Water (La balada del agua del mar) ... 21
Wish (Deseo) 23
Invocation to the Laurel (Invocación al laurel) 24

From: Poema del cante jondo, 1921 28
The Little Ballad of the Three Rivers (Baladilla de los tres ríos) ... 28
Landscape (Paisaje) 31
The Guitar (La guitarra) 32
The Footsteps of la Siguiriya (El paso de la siguiriya) 34
Cellar Song (Cueva) 35
Paso (The Images of the Passion) 36
Journey (Camino) 37
Lola (La Lola) 38
Village (Pueblo: poema de la soleá) 39
Juan Breva 40
Singing Café (Café cantante) 41
Malagueña 42

From: Primeras canciones, 1922 43
Variation (Variación) 43
Remanso, Final Song (Remanso, Canción final) 44
Captive (Cautiva) 45

From: Canciones, 1921-1924 46
Little Song of Seville (Cancioncilla sevillana) 46
Adelina Walking By (Adelina de paseo) 48
Song of the Rider (Canción del jinete) 50
It's True (Es verdad) 51
Tree, Tree (Arbolé, arbolé) 52
Prince (Galán) 54
Venus 55
The Moon Wakes (La luna asoma) 56
Two Moons of Evening (Dos lunas de tarde) 57
Second Anniversary (Segundo aniversario) 59
Schematic Nocturne (Nocturno esquemático) 59
Lucía Martínez 60
Farewell (Despedida) 61
Little Song of First Desire (Cancioncilla del primer deseo) 62
Prelude (Preludio) 63
Song of the Barren Orange Tree (Canción del Naranjo seco) 64
Serenade (Serenata) 65
Sonnet (Soneto) 66

From: Poemas sueltos (Uncollected poems) 67
Every Song (Cada canción) 67
Earth (Terra) 68
Berceuse for a Mirror Sleeping (Berceuse al Espejo dormido) 69
Ode to Salvador Dalí (Oda a Salvador Dalí) 70
Night-Song of the Andalusian Sailors (Canto nocturno de los marineros andaluces)
.... 75
Running (Corriente) 77
Towards (Hacia) 78
Return (Recodo) 79
Flash of Light (Ráfaga) 80
Madrigals (Madrigales) 81
The Garden (El Jardín) 82
Print of the Garden II (Estampas del jardín II) 84
Song of the Boy with Seven Hearts (Cancíon del muchacho de siete corazones) .. 86

The Dune (Duna) 87
Encounter (Encuentro) 88
Two Laws (Normas) 90
Sonnet (Soneto) 91

From: Gypsy Ballads (Romancero Gitano), 1924-1927 92
Romance de la Luna, Luna 92
Preciosa and the Breeze (Preciosa y el aire) 95
The Quarrel (Reyerta) 98
Romance Sonámbulo 100
The Gypsy Nun (La monja gitana) 104
The Unfaithful Wife (La casada infiel) 106
Ballad of the Black Sorrow (Romance de la pena negra) 109
Saint Michael (San Miguel) 111
Saint Gabriel (San Gabriel) 114
Romance of the Spanish Civil Guard (Romance de la Guardia Civil española) .. 117
Thamar and Amnon (Thamar y Amnón) 123

From: Poet in New York (Poeta en Nueva York), 1929-1930 127
The Dawn (La aurora) 127
Double Poem of Lake Eden (Poema doble del lago Edén) 129
Death 132
Ode to Walt Whitman 133
The Poet Arrives in Havana (El poeta llega a la Habana) 140

From: Bodas de sangre: Blood Wedding: Act I: 1933 142
Lullaby of the Great Stallion (Nana del caballo grande) 142

From: Llanto por Ignacio Sánchez Mejías, 1935 145
Lament for Ignacio Sánchez Mejías 145

From: Six Galician Poems (Seis poemas Gallegos), 1935 156
Madrigal for the City of Santiago 156
Nocturne of the Drowned Youth 157
Dance of the Santiago Moon 158

From: The Tamarit Divan (Diván del Tamarit), 1936 160
Ghazal of Unexpected Love (Gacela del amor imprevisto) 160
Ghazal of the Terrible Presence (Gacela de la terrible presencia) 161
Ghazal of the Bitter Root (Gacela de la raíz amarga) 162
Ghazal of the Flight (Gacela de la huida) 163
Ghazal of Dark Death (Gacela de la muerte oscura) 164
Casida of One Wounded by Water (Casida del herido por el agua) 165
Casida of the Weeping (Casida del llanto) 167
Casida of the Branches (Casida de los ramos) 168
Casida of the Recumbent Woman (Casida de la mujer tendida) 169
Casida of the Impossible Hand (Casida de la mano imposible) 170
Casida of the Rose (Casida de la Rosa) 171
Casida of the Golden Girl (Casida de la muchacha dorada) 172
Casida of the Dark Doves (Casida de las palomas oscuras) 174

From: Sonnets of Dark Love (Sonetos del amor oscuro), 1936 175
Wounds of Love (Llagas de amor) 175
Sonnet of the Wreath of Roses (Soneto de la guirnalda de las rosas) 176
The Poet asks his Love to write (El poeta pide a su amor que le escribe) 177
O Secret Voice of Hidden Love! (Ay voz secreta del amor oscuro!) 178
Sonnet of the Sweet Complaint (Soneto de la dulce queja) 179
Night of Insomniac Love 180
The Beloved Sleeps on the Breast of the Poet (El amor duerme en el pecho de poeta) 181

Index of First Lines 183

About the Translator 186

Translator's Introduction

Federico García Lorca (1898-1936), poet, playwright, and theatre director was a member of the early twentieth century group of Spanish poets who introduced the tenets of European movements (including symbolism, futurism, and surrealism) to Spanish literature. He was born in Fuente Vaqueros, near Granada, and educated in Granada and Madrid, where he befriended Dalí, Buñuel and Jiménez. His work became widely known on the publication of *Romancero gitano* (*Gypsy Ballads*, 1928), which incorporated themes and motifs from his native Andalusia, in a stylistically avant-garde manner. After his visit to the Americas, and New York City (1929 -1930), the latter recalled in the poems of *Poeta en Nueva York* (*Poet in New York*, 1942) Lorca returned to Spain where he wrote his later plays, *Blood Wedding* (1932), *Yerma* (1934), and *The House of Bernarda Alba* (1936).

The poet was executed by Nationalist forces at the beginning of the Spanish Civil War. His remains have not been found, while the motive for his death remains in dispute; speculatively it was aroused by his sexual orientation, his politics, or both, while a personal dispute nonetheless remains a strong possibility.

Lorca's poetry appeals through its immediacy, its skilful exploitation of the vibrant Spanish language, its transmission of iconic elements of Andalusian culture, and its emotional intensity and honesty. Its apparent simplicity is often deceptive, while its resonances are moving and profound; though, truly, little can be said of it that is not better expressed by the poems themselves.

Federico García Lorca

From: Libro de Poemas, 1921

Weather-Vane (*Veleta*)

(July 1920, Fuente Vaqueros, Granada)

Wind of the South.
Dark-haired, ardent,
you come over my flesh
bringing me seed
of brilliant
gazes, soaked
in orange blossom.

You make the moon red
and make a sobbing
in the captive poplars, but you come
too late!
I've rolled up the night of my story
on the shelf!

Without any wind,
Look out!
Spin, heart;
spin, heart.
    Breeze of the North,

From: Libro de Poemas, 1921

white bear of the wind!
you come over my flesh
trembling with auroras
boreales,
with your cloak
of spectral captains
and screaming with laughter
at Dante.
O polisher of stars!
But you come
too late.
My chest is covered with moss
and I've lost the key.

    Without any wind,
Look out!
Spin, heart;
spin, heart.

Gnomish airs, and winds
from nowhere.
Mosquitoes of the rose
with pyramidal petals,
Trade winds weaned
among the rough trees,
flutes in the tempest,
leave me be!
Strong chains hold

my memory,
and the bird is captive
whose warbling draws
the evening.

The things that are gone never return,
all the world knows that,
and among the clear crowd of the winds
it's useless to complain.
Isn't that so, poplar, master of the breeze?
It's useless to complain!

    Without any wind,
Look out!
Spin, heart;
spin, heart.

From: Libro de Poemas, 1921

New Songs
(*Cantos Nuevos*)

The afternoon speaks: 'I am thirsty for shadows!'
The moon speaks: 'I thirst for stars.'
The crystalline fountain asks for lips
and the wind for sighs.

I am thirsty for perfumes and laughter.
I thirst for new songs
without moons or irises,
and without loves that have died.

A song of the morning that might tremble
the quiet still pools
of the future. And fill with hope
their waves and mud.

A song, luminous and restful,
full of pensiveness,
innocent of miseries and anguish,
innocent of dream.

A song without lyric substance that fills
the silence with laughter.
(A flock of blind doves
thrown into mystery.)

Federico García Lorca

A song that might go to the soul of things
and to the soul of the winds
and that might rest at last in the joy
of the eternal heart.

From: Libro de Poemas, 1921

Dream (*Sueño*)

My heart rests, by the cold fountain.
    (Fill it with threads,
    spider of silence.)

The fountain-water sang it the song.
    (Fill it with threads,
    spider of silence.)

My heart, waking, sang its desires.
    (Spider of nothingness,
    spin your mystery.)

The fountain-water listened sombrely.
    (Spider of nothingness,
    spin your mystery.)

My heart falls into the cold of the fountain.
    (White hands, far-out,
    hold back the water.)

The water carries it, singing with joy.
    (White hands, far-out,
    nothing there in the water!)

Federico García Lorca

Spanish Fountain (1912)
John Singer Sargent (American, 1856-1925)
Artvee

From: Libro de Poemas, 1921

Ballad of the Small Plaza
(*Balada de la placate*)

Singing of children
in the night silence:
Light of the stream, and
calm of the fountain!

    THE CHILDREN

  What does your heart hold,
  divine in its gladness?

    MYSELF

  A peal from the bell-tower,
  lost in the dimness.

    THE CHILDREN

  You leave us singing
  in the small plaza.
  Light of the stream, and
  calm of the fountain!

  What do you hold in
  your hands of springtime?

MYSELF

A rose of blood, and
a lily of whiteness.

THE CHILDREN

Dip them in water
of the song of the ages.
Light of the stream, and
calm of the fountain!

What does your tongue feel,
scarlet and thirsting?

MYSELF

A taste of the bones
of my giant forehead.

THE CHILDREN

Drink the still water
of the song of the ages.
Light of the stream, and
calm of the fountain!

Why do you roam far
from the small plaza?

From: Libro de Poemas, 1921

MYSELF

I go to find Mages
and find princesses.

THE CHILDREN

Who showed you the road there,
the road of the poets?

MYSELF

The fount and the stream of
the song of the ages.

THE CHILDREN

Do you go far from
the earth and the ocean?

MYSELF

It's filled with light, is
my heart of silk, and
with bells that are lost,
with bees and with lilies,
and I will go far off,
behind those hills there,
close to the starlight,

to ask of the Christ there
Lord, to return me
my child's soul, ancient,
ripened with legends,
with a cap of feathers,
and a sword of wood.

THE CHILDREN

You leave us singing
in the small plaza.
Light of the stream, and
calm of the fountain!

Enormous pupils
of the parched palm fronds
hurt by the wind, they
weep their dead leaves.

From: Libro de Poemas, 1921

A Spanish Garden (1871)
Martin Rico y Ortega (Spanish, 1833-1908)
Artvee

Federico García Lorca

The Ballad of the Salt-Water
(*La balada del agua del mar*)

The sea
smiles far-off.
Spume-teeth,
sky-lips.

'What do you sell, troubled child,
child with naked breasts?'

'Sir, I sell
salt-waters of the sea.'

'What do you carry, dark child,
mingled with your blood?'

'Sir, I carry
salt-waters of the sea.'

'These tears of brine
where do they come from, mother?'

'Sir, I cry
salt-waters of the sea.'

'Heart, this deep bitterness,
where does it rise from?'

From: Libro de Poemas, 1921

'So bitter, the salt-waters
of the sea!'

The sea
smiles far-off.
Spume-teeth.
Sky-lips.

The Rock of Gibraltar from Algeciras (Spain) (1843)
George Lothian Hall (English, 1825-1888)
Artvee

Federico García Lorca

Wish (*Deseo*)

Just your hot heart,
nothing more.

My Paradise, a field,
no nightingales,
no strings,
a river, discrete,
and a little fountain.

Without the spurs,
of the wind, in the branches,
without the star,
that wants to be leaf.

An enormous light
that will be
the glow
of the Other,
in a field of broken gazes.

A still calm
where our kisses,
sonorous circles
of echoes,
will open, far-off.

And your hot heart,
nothing more.

From: Libro de Poemas, 1921

Invocation to the Laurel
(*Invocación al laurel*)

(*1919 For Pepe Cienfuegos*)

Over the horizon, lost in confusion,

came the sad night, pregnant with stars.

I, like the bearded mage of the tales,

knew the language of stones and flowers.

I learned the secrets of melancholy,

told by cypresses, nettles and ivy;

I knew the dream from lips of nard,

sang serene songs with the irises.

In the old forest, filled with its blackness,

all of them showed me the souls they have;

the pines, drunk on aroma and sound;

the old olives, burdened with knowledge;

the dead poplars, nests for the ants;

the moss, snowy with white violets.

All spoke tenderly to my heart

trembling in threads of rustling silk

where water involves motionless things,

like a web of eternal harmony.

The roses there were sounding the lyre,
oaks weaving the gold of legends,
and amidst their virile sadness
the junipers spoke of rustic fears.

I knew all the passion of woodland;
rhythms of leaves, rhythms of stars.
But tell me, oh cedars, if my heart
will sleep in the arms of perfect light!

I know the lyre you prophesy, roses:
fashioned of strings from my dead life.
Tell me what pool I might leave it in,
as former passions are left behind!

I know the mystery you sing of, cypress;
I am your brother of night and pain;
we hold inside us a tangle of nests,
you of nightingales, I of sadness!

I know your endless enchantment, old olive tree,
yielding us blood you extract from the Earth,
like you, I extract with my feelings
the sacred oil
held by ideas!

From: Libro de Poemas, 1921

You all overwhelm me with songs;
I ask only for my uncertain one;
none of you will quell the anxieties
of this chaste fire
that burns in my breast.

O laurel divine, with soul inaccessible,
always so silent,
filled with nobility!
Pour in my ears your divine history,
all your wisdom, profound and sincere!

Tree that produces fruits of the silence,
maestro of kisses and mage of orchestras,
formed from Daphne's roseate flesh
with Apollo's potent sap in your veins!

O high priest of ancient knowledge!
O solemn mute, closed to lament!
All your forest brothers speak to me;
only you, harsh one, scorn my song!

Perhaps, oh maestro of rhythm, you muse
on the pointlessness of the poet's sad weeping.
Perhaps your leaves, flecked by the moonlight,
forgo all the illusions of spring.

Federico García Lorca

The delicate tenderness of evening,

that covered the path with black dew,

holding out a vast canopy to night,

came solemnly, pregnant with stars.

From Sevilla in Spain (1882)
Christian Skredsvig (Norwegian, 1854 – 1924)
Artvee

From: Poema del cante jondo, 1921

The Little Ballad of the Three Rivers
(*Baladilla de los tres ríos*)

The Guadalquivir's stream
runs past oranges and olives.
The two rivers of Granada,
fall to wheat-fields, out of snow.

Ay, Love, that goes,
    and never returns!

The Guadalquivir's stream
    has a beard of clear garnet.
    The two rivers of Granada
    one of sorrow, one of blood.

Ay, Love,
    vanished down the wind!

For the sailing-boats,
Seville keeps a roadway:
Through the waters of Granada
only sighs can row.

Ay, Love, that went,
> and never returned!

Guadalquivir — high tower,
and breeze in the orange-trees.
Darro, Genil — dead turrets,
dead, above the ponds.

Ay, Love,
> vanished down the wind!

Who can say, if water carries
a ghost-fire of cries?

Ay, Love, that went,
> and never returned!

Take the orange petals,
take the leaves of olives,
Andalusia, down to your sea.

Ay, Love,
> vanished on the wind!

From: Poema del cante jondo, 1921

Alcazar, Segovia, Spain (1836)
David Roberts (Scottish, 1796-1864)
Artvee

Federico García Lorca

Landscape (*Paisaje*)

The field

of olives

opens and closes,

like a fan.

Over the olives,

deep sky,

and dark rain,

of frozen stars.

Reeds, and blackness,

tremble, by the river.

Grey air shivers.

The olives

are full of cries.

A crowd

of imprisoned birds,

moving long tails

in shadow.

From: Poema del cante jondo, 1921

The Guitar (*La guitarra*)

It begins, the lament

of the guitar.

The wineglass of dawn

is broken.

t begins, the lament

of the guitar.

It's useless to silence it.

Impossible

to silence it.

It cries monotonously

as the water cries,

as the wind cries

over the snow.

Impossible

to silence it.

It cries for

distant things.

Sands of the hot South

that demand white camellias.

It cries arrows with no targets,

evening with no morning,

and the first dead bird

on the branch.

Oh, the guitar!

Heart wounded deep

by five swords.

Federico García Lorca

Spanish Dance (1882)
Ernst Josephson (Swedish, 1851 - 1906)
Artvee

From: Poema del cante jondo, 1921

The Footsteps of la Siguiriya
(*El paso de la siguiriya*)

Through black butterflies
goes a girl with dark hair
joined to a white serpent
of mistiness.

Earth of light,
Sky of Earth.

She goes tied to the trembling
of a rhythm that never arrives:
she has a heart of silver
and a dagger in her hand.

'Where do you go, Siguiriya
with a mindless rhythm?
What moon will gather up your
grief of lime and oleander?

Earth of light,
Sky of Earth.

Note: La Siguiriya, is a gipsy song, a basic form of canto jondo, the 'deep song' of Andalusia. Its emotionally intense lyrics do not depend on rationality and are usually in four verse lines with assonant rhyme, and syllables 6-6-11-6.

Federico García Lorca

Cellar Song (Cueva)

From the cellar issue
great sobs.

(The purple
above the red.)

The gypsy evokes
distant countries.

(High towers and men
of mystery.)

On his faltering voice
his eyes travel.

(The black
above the red.)

And the whitewashed cellar
trembles in gold.

(The white
above the red.)

From: Poema del cante jondo, 1921

Paso (The Images of the Passion)

Virgin in a crinoline,
Virgin of Solitude,
spreading immensely
like a tulip-flower.

In your boat of light,
go –
through the high seas of the city.
through turbulent singing,
through crystalline stars.

Virgin in a crinoline
through the roadway's river
you go,
down to the sea!

Federico García Lorca

Journey (*Camino*)

A hundred riders in mourning,

where might they be going,

along the low horizon

of the orange grove?

They could not arrive

at Sevilla or Cordoba.

Nor at Granada, she who sighs

for the sea.

These drowsy horses

may carry them

to the labyrinth of crosses

where the singing trembles.

With seven nailed sighs,

where might they be going

the hundred Andalusian riders

of the orange-grove?

From: Poema del cante jondo, 1921

Lola (La Lola)

Under the orange-tree
she washes baby-clothes.
Her eyes of green
and voice of violet.

   Ay, love,
under the orange-tree in bloom!

The water in the ditch
flowed, filled with light,
a sparrow chirped
in the little olive-tree.

   Ay, love,
under the orange-tree in bloom!

Later, when Lola
has exhausted the soap,
young bullfighters will come.

   Ay, love,
under the orange-tree in bloom!

Federico García Lorca

Village (Pueblo: poema de la soleá)

A calvary,

on the naked hillside.

Clear water.

Centenarian olives.

Through the narrow alleys,

men with cloaks on,

and on turrets,

wind-vanes, circling.

Eternally

rotating.

O lost pueblo,

in Andalusia of sorrows!

From: Poema del cante jondo, 1921

Juan Breva

Juan Breva had
the body of a giant
and the voice of a young girl.
Nothing was like his warbling.
It was itself
pain singing
behind a smile.
He evoked the lemons
of Málaga, the sleepy one,
and had in his weeping tones
the brine of the ocean.
Like Homer, he sang
blind. His voice held
something of sea with no light
and an orange squeezed dry.

Federico García Lorca

Singing Café (*Café cantante*)

Lamps of crystal

and green mirrors.

On the dark stage

Parrala holds

a dialogue

with death.

Calls her,

she won't come,

Calls her again.

The people

swallow their sobbing.

And in the green mirrors

long trails of silk

move.

From: Poema del cante jondo, 1921

Malagueña

Death
enters, and leaves,
the tavern.

Black horses
and sinister people
travel the deep roads
of the guitar.

And there's a smell of salt
and of female blood
in the fevered tuberoses
of the shore.

Death
enters and leaves,
and leaves and enters
the death
of the tavern.

Federico García Lorca

From: Primeras canciones, 1922

Variation (*Variación*)

The *remanso* of air
under the branch of echo.

The *remanso* of water
under a frond of stars.

The *remanso* of your mouth
under a thicket of kisses.

Note. A remanso is a still pool in a running stream.

From: Primeras canciones, 1922

Remanso, Final Song
(Remanso, Canción final)

The night is coming.

The moonlight strikes
on evening's anvil.

The night is coming.

A giant tree clothes itself
in the leaves of cantos.

The night is coming.

If you came to see me,
on the path of storm-winds...

The night is coming.

...you would find me crying,
under high, black poplars.
Ay, girl with the dark hair!
Under high, black poplars.

Federico García Lorca

Captive (*Cautiva*)

Through the indecisive
branches
went a girl
who was life.
Through the indecisive
branches.
She reflected daylight,
with a tiny mirror,
which was the splendour,
of her unclouded forehead.
Through the indecisive
branches.
In the dark of night,
lost, she wandered,
weeping the dew,
of this imprisoned time.
Through the indecisive
branches.

From: Canciones, 1921-1924

Little Song of Seville (*Cancioncilla sevillana*)

At the dawn of day
in the orange grove.
Little bees of gold
searching for honey.

Where is the honey
then?

It's in the flower of blue,
Isabel.
In the flower
there, of rosemary.

(A little gold chair,
for the Moor,
A tinsel chair,
for his spouse.)

At the dawn of day
in the orange grove.

Federico García Lorca

From Sevilla in Spain (1882)
Christian Skredsvig (Norwegian, 1854 – 1924)
Artvee

From: Canciones, 1921-1924

Adelina Walking By (*Adelina de paseo*)

The sea has no oranges,
Sevilla has no love.
Dark-haired girl, what fiery light.
Lend me your parasol.

It will give me green cheeks
- juice of lime and lemon -
Your words – little fishes –
will swim all around us.

The sea has no oranges.
Ay, love.
Sevilla has no love!

Federico García Lorca

Palm Sunday in Spain (1873)
Jehan Georges Vibert (French, 1840 – 1902)
Artvee

From: Canciones, 1921-1924

Song of the Rider (*Canción del jinete*)

Córdoba.
Far away, and lonely.

Full moon, black pony,
olives against my saddle.
Though I know all the roadways
I'll never get to Córdoba.

Through the breezes, through the valley,
red moon, black pony.
Death is looking at me
from the towers of Córdoba.

Ay, how long the road is!
Ay, my brave pony!
Ay, death is waiting for me,
before I get to Córdoba.

Córdoba.
Far away, and lonely.

Federico García Lorca

It's True (*Es verdad*)

Ay, the pain it costs me
to love you as I love you!

For love of you, the air, it hurts,
and my heart,
and my hat, they hurt me.

Who would buy it from me,
this ribbon I am holding,
and this sadness of cotton,
white, for making handkerchiefs with?

Ay, the pain it costs me
to love you as I love you!

From: Canciones, 1921-1924

Tree, Tree (Arbolé, arbolé)

Sapling, sapling,

Dry and green.

The girl with the lovely face,

goes, gathering olives.

The wind, that towering lover,

takes her by the waist.

Four riders go by

on Andalusian ponies,

in azure and emerald suits,

in long cloaks of shadow.

'Come to Cordoba, sweetheart!'

The girl does not listen.

Three young bullfighters go by,

slim-waisted in suits of orange,

with swords of antique silver.

'Come to Sevilla, sweetheart!'

The girl does not listen.

When the twilight purples,

with the daylight's dying,

a young man goes by, holding

roses, and myrtle of moonlight.

'Come to Granada, my sweetheart!'

But the girl does not listen.

The girl, with the lovely face,

goes on gathering olives,

while the wind's grey arms
go circling her waist.

Sapling, sapling,
Dry and green.

From: Canciones, 1921-1924

Prince (*Galán*)

Prince,

little prince.

In your house they're burning thyme.

Whether you're going, whether you're coming,

I will lock the door with a key.

With a key of pure silver.

Tied up with a ribbon.

On the ribbon there's a message:

My heart is far away.

Don't pace up and down my street.

All that's allowed there is the wind!

Prince,

little prince.

In your house they're burning thyme.

Federico García Lorca

Venus

(*So, I saw you*)

The young girl dead
in the seashell of the bed,
naked of flowers and breezes
rose in the light unending.

The world was left behind,
lily of cotton and shadows,
revealing in crystal panes
the infinite transit's coming.

The young girl dead,
ploughed love inside.
Among the foaming sheets
her hair was wasted.

From: Canciones, 1921-1924

The Moon Wakes (*La luna asoma*)

When the moon sails out
the bells fade into stillness
and there emerge the pathways
that can't be penetrated.

When the moon sails out
the water hides earth's surface,
the heart feels like an island
in the infinite silence.

Nobody eats an orange
under the moon's fullness.
It is correct to eat, then,
green and icy fruit.

When the moon sails out
with a hundred identical faces,
the coins made of silver
sob in your pocket.

Federico García Lorca

Two Moons of Evening
(*Dos lunas de tarde*)

(*For Laurita, friend of my sister*)

I

The Moon is dying, dying:
but will be born again in the spring.

When on the brow of the poplars
is curled the wind from the south.

When our hearts have given
their harvest of sighing.

When the rooftops are wearing
their little sombreros of weeds.

The moon is dying, dying:
but will be reborn in the spring.

II

(*For Isabelita, my sister*)

The evening is chanting
a *berceuse* to the oranges.

From: Canciones, 1921-1924

My little sister's chanting:
the Earth is an orange.

The moon weeping cries:
I want to be an orange.

You cannot be, my child,
even if you were reddened.
Not even if you turned lemon.
What a shame that is!

Note: A berceuse is a French cradle-song.

Federico García Lorca

Second Anniversary (*Segundo aniversario*)

The moon lays a long horn,
of light, on the sea.

Tremoring, ecstatic,
the grey-green unicorn.

The sky floats over the wind,
a huge flower of lotus.

(O you, walking alone,
in the last house of night!)

Schematic Nocturne (*Nocturno esquemático*)

The fennel, a serpent, and rushes.
Aroma, a sign, and penumbra.
Air, earth, and solitariness.

(The ladder lifts up to the moon.)

From: Canciones, 1921-1924

Lucía Martínez

Lucía Martínez.
Shadowy in red silk.

Your thighs, like the evening,
go from light to shadow.
The hidden veins of jet
darken your magnolias.

Here I am, Lucía Martínez.
I come to devour your mouth
and drag you off by the hair
into the dawn of conches.

Because I want to, because I can.
Shadowy in red silk.

Federico García Lorca

Farewell (*Despedida*)

If I should die,
leave the balcony open.

The child is eating an orange.
(From my balcony, I see him.)

The reaper is reaping the barley.
(From my balcony, I hear him.)

If I should die,
leave the balcony open.

From: Canciones, 1921-1924

Little Song of First Desire
(*Cancioncilla del primer deseo*)

In the green morning
I wanted to be a heart.
Heart.

And in the ripe evening
I wanted to be a nightingale.
Nightingale.

(Soul,
go the colour of oranges.
Soul
go the colour of love.)

In the living morning
I wanted to be me.
Heart.

And at evening's fall
I wanted to be my voice.
Nightingale.

Soul
go the colour of oranges.
Soul,
go the colour of love!

Federico García Lorca

Prelude (*Preludio*)

(From Amor: with wings and arrows)

The poplar groves are going,
but leave us their reflection.

The poplar groves are going,
but leave us the breeze.

The breeze is shrouded
full length below the heavens.

But it has left there, floating,
its echoes on the rivers.

The world of the glow-worms
has pierced my memories.

And the tiniest of hearts
buds from my fingertips.

From: Canciones, 1921-1924

Song of the Barren Orange Tree
(*Canción del Naranjo seco*)

Woodcutter.

Cut out my shadow.

Free me from the torture

of seeing myself fruitless.

Why was I born among mirrors?

The daylight revolves around me.

And the night herself repeats me

in all her constellations.

I want to live not seeing self.

I shall dream the husks and insects

change inside my dreaming

into my birds and foliage.

Woodcutter.

Cut out my shadow.

Free me from the torture

of seeing myself fruitless.

Federico García Lorca

Serenade (*Serenata*)

(*Homage to Lope de Vega*)

By the river banks
the night is moistening itself
and on Lolita's breasts
the branches die of love.

    The branches die of love.

The naked night sings
over the March bridgeheads.
Lolita washes her body
with brine and tuberoses.

    The branches die of love.

The night of aniseed and silver
shines on the rooftops.
Silver of streams and mirrors.
Aniseed of your white thighs.

    The branches die of love.

From: Canciones, 1921-1924

Sonnet (*Soneto*)

A long ghost of silver moving
the night-wind's sighing
opened my old hurt with its grey hand
and moved on: I was left yearning.

Wound of love that will grant my life
endless blood and pure welling light.
Cleft in which Philomel, struck dumb,
will find her grove, her grief and tender nest.

Ay, what sweet murmurs in my head!
I'll lie down by the single flower
where your beauty floats without a soul.

And the wandering waters will turn yellow,
as my blood runs through the moist
and fragrant undergrowth of the shore.

From: Poemas sueltos (Uncollected poems)

Every Song (*Cada canción*)

Every song
is the remains
of love.

Every light
the remains
of time.
A knot
of time.

And every sigh
the remains
of a cry.

From: Poemas sueltos (Uncollected poems)

Earth (*Terra*)

We travel

over a mirror

without silver,

over a crystal

without cloud.

If the lilies were to grow

upside down,

is the roses were to grow

upside down,

if all the roots

were to face the stars

and the dead not shut

their eyes,

we would be like swans.

Federico García Lorca

Berceuse for a Mirror Sleeping
(*Berceuse al Espejo dormido*)

  Sleep.
Do not fear the gaze
that wanders.
  Sleep.

Not the butterfly
or the word
or the furtive ray
from the keyhole
will hurt you.
  Sleep.

As my heart
so, you,
mirror of mine.
Garden where love
awaits me.

Sleep without a care,
but wake
when the last one dies
the kiss on my lips.

From: Poemas sueltos (Uncollected poems)

Ode to Salvador Dalí (*Oda a Salvador Dalí*)

A rose in the high garden that you desire.
A wheel in the pure syntax of steel.
The mountain stripped of impressionist mist.
Greys looking out from the last balustrades.

Modern painters in their blank studios,
Sever the square root's sterilized flower.
In the Seine's flood an iceberg of marble
freezes the windows and scatters the ivy.

Man treads the paved streets firmly.
Crystals hide from reflections' magic.
Government has closed the perfume shops.
The machine beats out its binary rhythm.

An absence of forests, screens and brows
Wanders the roof-tiles of ancient houses.
The air polishes its prism on the sea
and the horizon looms like a vast aqueduct.

Marines ignorant of wine and half-light,
decapitate sirens on seas of lead.
Night, black statue of prudence, holds
the moon's round mirror in her hand.

Federico García Lorca

A desire for form and limit conquers us.
Here comes the man who sees with a yellow ruler.
Venus is a white still life
and the butterfly collectors flee.

Cadaqués, the fulcrum of water and hill,
lifts flights of steps and hides seashells.
Wooden flutes pacify the air.
An old god of the woods gives children fruit.

Her fishermen slumber, dreamless, on sand.
On the deep, a rose serves as their compass.
The virgin horizon of wounded handkerchiefs,
unites the vast crystals of fish and moon.

A hard diadem of white brigantines
wreathes bitter brows and hair of sand.
The sirens convince, but fail to beguile,
and appear if we show a glass of fresh water.

O Salvador Dalí, of the olive voice!
I don't praise your imperfect adolescent brush
or your pigments that circle those of your age,
I salute your yearning for bounded eternity.

Healthy soul, you live on fresh marble.
You flee the dark wood of improbable forms.
Your fantasy reaches as far as your hands,
and you savor the sea's sonnet at your window.

From: Poemas sueltos (Uncollected poems)

The world holds dull half-light and disorder,
in the foreground humanity frequents.
But now the stars, concealing landscapes,
mark out the perfect scheme of their courses.

The flow of time forms pools, gains order,
in the measured forms of age upon age.
And conquered Death, trembling, takes refuge
in the straightened circle of the present moment.

Taking your palette, its wing holds a bullet-hole,
you summon the light that revives the olive-tree.
Broad light of Minerva, builder of scaffolding,
with no room for dream and its inexact flower.

You summon the light that rests on the brow,
not reaching the mouth or the heart of man.
Light feared by the trailing vines of Bacchus,
and the blind force driving the falling water.

You do well to place warning flags
on the dark frontier that shines with night.
As a painter you don't wish your forms softened
by the shifting cotton of unforeseen clouds.

The fish in its bowl and the bird in its cage.
You refuse to invent them in sea or in air.
You stylize or copy once you have seen,
with your honest eyes, their small agile bodies.

Federico García Lorca

You love a matter defined and exact,
where the lichen cannot set up its camp.
You love architecture built on the absent,
admitting the banner merely in jest.

The steel compass speaks its short flexible verse.
Now unknown islands deny the sphere.
The straight line speaks of its upward fight
and learned crystals sing their geometry.

Yet the rose too in the garden where you live.
Ever the rose, ever, our north and south!
Calm, intense like an eyeless statue,
blind to the underground struggle it causes.

Pure rose that frees from artifice, sketches,
and opens for us the slight wings of a smile.
(Pinned butterfly that muses in flight.)
Rose of pure balance not seeking pain.
Ever the rose!

O Salvador Dalí of the olive voice!
I speak of what you and your paintings tell me.
I don't praise your imperfect adolescent brush,
but I sing the firm aim of your arrows.

From: Poemas sueltos (Uncollected poems)

I sing your sweet battle of Catalan lights,
your love of what might be explained.
I sing your heart astronomical, tender,
a deck of French cards, and never wounded.

I sing longing for statues, sought without rest,
your fear of emotions that wait in the street.
I sing the tiny sea-siren who sings to you
riding a bicycle of corals and conches.

But above all I sing a shared thought
that joins us in the dark and golden hours.
It is not Art, this light that blinds our eyes.
Rather it is love, friendship, the clashing of swords.

Rather than the picture you patiently trace,
it's the breast of Theresa, she of insomniac skin,
the tight curls of Mathilde the ungrateful,
our friendship a board-game brightly painted.

May the tracks of fingers in blood on gold
stripe the heart of eternal Catalonia.
May stars like fists without falcons shine on you,
while your art and your life burst into flower.

Don't watch the water-clock with membranous wings,
nor the harsh scythe of the allegories.
Forever clothe and bare your brush in the air
before the sea peopled with boats and sailors.

Federico García Lorca

Night-Song of the Andalusian Sailors
(*Canto nocturno de los marineros andaluces*)

From Cádiz to Gibraltar
how fine the road!
The sea knows I go by,
by the sighs.

Ay, girl of mine, girl of mine,
how full of boats is Málaga harbour!

From Cádiz to Sevilla
how many little lemons!
The lemon-trees know me,
by the sighs.

Ay, girl of mine, girl of mine,
how full of boats is Málaga harbour!

From Sevilla to Carmona
there isn't a single knife.
The half-moon slices,
and, wounded, the air goes by.

Ay, boy of mine, boy of mine,
let the waves carry off my stallion!

From: Poemas sueltos (Uncollected poems)

Through the pale salt-seams
I forgot you, my love.
He who needs a heart
let him ask for my forgetting.

Ay, boy of mine, boy of mine,
let the waves carry off my stallion!

Cádiz, let the sea flow over you,
don't advance this way.
Sevilla, on your feet,
so, you don't drown in the river.

Ay, girl of mine!
Ay, boy of mine!
How fine the road!
How full of boats the harbour,
and how cold it is in the square!

Merida, Spain
John Varley (English, 1778-1842)
Artvee

Federico García Lorca

Running (*Corriente*)

That which travels
clouds itself.

The flowing water
can see no stars.

That which travels
forgets itself.

And that which halts itself
dreams.

From: Poemas sueltos (Uncollected poems)

Towards (*Hacia*)

    Turn,

    Heart!

    Turn.

Through the woods of love
you will see no one.
You will pour out bright fountains.
In the green
you will find the immense rose
of Always.

And you will say: 'Love! Love!
without your wound
being closed.

    Turn,

    Heart!

    Turn.

Federico García Lorca

Return (*Recodo*)

I want to return to childhood
and from childhood to the shadows.

>Are you going, nightingale?
>Go!

I want to return to the shadows,
and from the shadows to the flower.

>Are you going, fragrance?
>Go!

I want to return to the flower
and from the flower
to my heart.

>Are you going, love?
>Farewell!

(To my abandoned heart!)

From: Poemas sueltos (Uncollected poems)

Flash of Light (Ráfaga)

She passes by, my girl.
How prettily she goes by!
With her little dress
of muslin.
And a captive
butterfly.

Follow her, my boy, then
up every byway!
And if you see her weeping
or weighing things up, then
paint her heart over
with a bit of purple
and tell her not to weep if
she was left single.

Federico García Lorca

Madrigals (*Madrigales*)

I

Like concentric ripples
over the water,
so, in my heart
your words.

Like a bird that strikes
against the wind,
so, on my lips
your kisses.

Like exposed fountains
opposing the evening,
so, my dark eyes
over your flesh.

II

I am caught
in your circles,
concentric.
Like Saturn
I wear
the rings
of my dream.
I am not ruined by setting
nor do I rise myself.

From: Poemas sueltos (Uncollected poems)

The Garden (*El Jardín*)

Never born, never!
But could come into bud.

Every second it
is deepened and renewed.

Every second opens
new distinct pathways.

This way! That way!
Go my multiplying bodies.

Traversing the villages
or sleeping in the sea.

Everything is open! There are
locks for the keys.
But the sun and moon
lose us and mislead us.
And beneath our feet
the roadways are confused.

Here I'll contemplate
all I could have been.
God or beggar,
water or ancient pearl.

My many pathways
lightly tinted
make a vast rose
round my body.

Like a map, but impossible,
the garden of the possible.
Every second it
is deepened and renewed.

Never born, never!
But could come into bud.

From: Poemas sueltos (Uncollected poems)

Print of the Garden II
(*Estampas del jardín II*)

The Moon-widow
who could forget her?
Dreaming that Earth
might be crystal.

Furious and pallid
wishing the sea to sleep
combing her long hair
with cries of coral.

Her tresses of glass
who could forget them?
In her breast the hundred
lips of a fountain.

Spears of giant
surges guard her
by the still waves
of sea-flats.

But the Moon, Moon
when will she return?
The curtain of wind
trembles without ceasing.

Federico García Lorca

The Moon-widow
who could forget her?
Dreaming that Earth
might be crystal.

From: Poemas sueltos (Uncollected poems)

Song of the Boy with Seven Hearts
(*Canción del muchacho de siete corazones*)

Seven hearts
I hold.
But mine does not encounter them.

In the high mountains, mother,
the wind and I ran into each other.
Seven young girls with long fingers
carried me on their mirrors.

I have sung through the world
with my mouth of seven petals.
My galleys of amaranth
have gone without ropes or oars.

I have lived in the lands
of others, My secrets
round my throat,
without my realising it, were open!

In the high mountains, mother,
(my heart above the echoes
in the album of a star)
the wind and I ran into each other.

Seven hearts
I hold.
But mine does not encounter them.

Federico García Lorca

The Dune (*Duna*)

On the wide sand-dune
of ancient light
I found myself confused
without a sky or road.

The moribund North
had quenched its stars.
The shipwrecked skies
rippled slowly.

Through the sea of light
where do I go? Whom do I seek?
Here the reflection wails
of veiled moons.

Ay! Let my cool sliver
of solid timber
return me to my balcony
and my living birds!

The garden will follow
shifting its borders
on the rough back
of a grounded silence.

From: Poemas sueltos (Uncollected poems)

Encounter (*Encuentro*)

Flower of sunlight.
Flower of water.

Myself: Was that you, with breasts of fire,
so that I could not see you?

She: How many times did they brush you,
the ribbons of my dress?

Myself: In your sealed throat, I hear
white voices, of my children.

She: Your children swim in my eyes,
like pale diamonds.

Myself: Was that you, my love? Where were you,
trailing infinite clouds of hair?

She: In the Moon. You smile? Well then,
round the flower of Narcissus.

Myself: In my chest, preventing sleep,
a serpent of ancient kisses.

She: The moment fell open, and settled
its roots on my sighs.

Federico García Lorca

Myself: Joined by the one breeze, face to face,
we did not know each other!

She: The branches are thickening, go now.
Neither of us two has been born!

    Flower of sunlight.
    Flower of water.

From: Poemas sueltos (Uncollected poems)

Two Laws (*Normas*)

Sketch of the Moon

The law of the past encountered
in my present night.
Splendour of adolescence
that opposes snowfall.
My two children of secrecy
cannot yield you a place,
dark-haired moon-girls of air
with exposed hearts.
But my love seeks the garden
where your spirit does not die.

Sketch of the Sun

Law of hip and breast
under the outstretched branch,
ancient and newly born
power of the Spring.
Now, bee, my nakedness wants
to be the dahlia of your fate,
the murmur or wine
of your madness and number:
but my love looks for the pure
madness of breeze and warbling.

Federico García Lorca

Sonnet (*Soneto*)

I know that my outline will be tranquil
in the north-wind of a sky without reflections,
mercury of watching, chaste mirror
where the pulse of my spirit is broken.

Because if ivy and the coolness of linen
are the law of the body I leave behind,
my outline in the sand will be the ancient
unembarrassed silence of the crocodile.

And though my tongue of frozen doves
will never hold the flavour of flame,
only the lost taste of broom,

I'll be the free sign of laws forced
on the neck of the stiff branch
and the endless aching dahlias.

From: Gypsy Ballads (Romancero Gitano), 1924-1927

From: Gypsy Ballads (Romancero Gitano), 1924-1927

Romance de la Luna, Luna

The moon comes to the forge,
in her creamy-white petticoat.
The child stares, stares.
The child is staring at her.
In the breeze, stirred,
the moon stirs her arms
shows, pure, voluptuous,
her breasts of hard tin.

'Away, Luna, Luna, Luna.
If the gypsies come here,
they'll take your heart for
necklaces and white rings.'
'Child, let me dance now.
When the gypsies come here,
they'll find you on the anvil,
with your little eyes closed.'
'Away, Luna, Luna, Luna,
because I hear their horses.'
'Child, go, but do not tread
on my starched whiteness.'

Federico García Lorca

The riders are coming nearer
beating on the plain, drumming.
Inside the forge, the child
has both his eyes closed.

Through the olive trees they come,
bronze, and dream, the gypsies,
their heads held upright,
their eyes half-open.

How the owl is calling.
Ay, it calls in the branches!
Through the sky goes the moon,
gripping a child's fingers.

In the forge the gypsies
are shouting and weeping.
The breeze guards, guards.
The breeze guards it.

From: Gypsy Ballads (Romancero Gitano), 1924-1927

Spanish Peasants Dancing the Bolero (1836)
John Frederick Lewis (English, 1805-1876)
Artvee

Federico García Lorca

Preciosa and the Breeze (*Preciosa y el aire*)

Preciosa comes playing
her moon of parchment
on an amphibious path
of crystals and laurels.
The silence without stars
fleeing from the sound,
falls to the sea that pounds and sings,
its night filled with fish.
On the peaks of the sierra
the carabineers are sleeping
guarding the white turrets
where the English live.
And the gypsies of the water
build, to amuse themselves,
bowers, out of snails
and twigs of green pine.

Preciosa comes playing
her moon of parchment.
Seeing her, the wind rises,
the one that never sleeps.
Saint Christopher, naked
full of celestial tongues
gazes at the child playing
a sweet distracted piping.

From: Gypsy Ballads (Romancero Gitano), 1924-1927

— Child, let me lift your dress
so that I can see you.
Open the blue rose of your womb
with my ancient fingers.

Preciosa hurls her tambourine
and runs without stopping.
The man-in-the-wind pursues her
with a burning sword.

The sea gathers its murmurs.
The olive-trees whiten.
The flutes of the shadows sound,
and the smooth gong of the snow.

Run, Preciosa, run,
lest the green wind catch you!
Run, Preciosa, run!
See where he comes!
The satyr of pale stars
with his shining tongues.

Preciosa, full of fear,
way beyond the pines,
enters the house that belongs,
to the English Consul.

Alarmed at her cries
three carabineers come,
their black capes belted,
and their caps over their brows.

The Englishman gives the gypsy girl
a glass of lukewarm milk,
and a cup of gin that
Preciosa does not drink.

And while, with tears, she tells
those people of her ordeal,
the angry wind bites the air
above the roofs of slate.

From: Gypsy Ballads (Romancero Gitano), 1924-1927

The Quarrel (*Reyerta*)

In mid-ravine
the Albacete knives
lovely with enemy blood
shine like fishes.
A hard light of playing-cards
silhouettes on the sharp green
angry horses
and profiles of riders.
In the heart of an olive-tree
two old women grieve.
The bull of the quarrel
climbs the walls.
Black angels bring
wet snow and handkerchiefs.
Angels with vast wings
like Albacete knives.
Juan Antonio of Montilla,
dead, rolls down the slope,
his corpse covered with lilies
and a pomegranate on his brow.
Now he mounts a cross of fire
on the roadway of death.

The judge, with the civil guard,
comes through the olives.
The slippery blood moans
a mute serpent song.
'Gentlemen of the civil guard:
here it is as always.
We have four dead Romans
and five Carthaginians.'

The afternoon delirious
with figs and heated murmurs,
fainted on the horsemen's
wounded thighs.
And black angels flew
on the west wind.
Angels with long tresses
and hearts of oil.

From: Gypsy Ballads (Romancero Gitano), 1924-1927

Romance Sonámbulo

Green, as I love you, greenly.
Green the wind, and green the branches.
The dark ship on the sea
and the horse on the mountain.
With her waist that's made of shadow
dreaming on the high veranda,
green the flesh, and green the tresses,
with eyes of frozen silver.
Green, as I love you, greenly.
Beneath the moon of the gypsies
silent things are looking at her
things she cannot see.

Green, as I love you, greenly.
Great stars of white hoarfrost
come with the fish of shadow
opening the road of morning.
The fig tree's rubbing on the dawn wind
with the rasping of its branches,
and the mountain thieving-cat-like
bristles with its sour agaves.
Who is coming? And from where...?
She waits on the high veranda,
green the flesh and green the tresses,
dreaming of the bitter ocean.

Federico García Lorca

'Brother, friend, I want to barter
your house for my stallion,
sell my saddle for your mirror,
change my dagger for your blanket.
Brother mine, I come here bleeding
from the mountain pass of Cabra.'
'If I could, my young friend,
then maybe we'd strike a bargain,
but I am no longer I,
nor is this house, of mine, mine.'
'Brother, friend, I want to die now,
in the fitness of my own bed,
made of iron, if it can be,
with its sheets of finest cambric.
Can you see the wound I carry
from my throat to my heart?'
'Three hundred red roses
your white shirt now carries.
Your blood stinks and oozes,
all around your scarlet sashes.
But I am no longer I,
nor is this house of mine, mine.'
'Let me then, at least, climb up there,
up towards the high verandas.
Let me climb, let me climb there,
up towards the green verandas.
High verandas of the moonlight,
where I hear the sound of waters.'

From: Gypsy Ballads (Romancero Gitano), 1924-1927

Now they climb, the two companions,
up there to the high veranda,
letting fall a trail of blood drops,
letting fall a trail of tears.
On the morning rooftops,
trembled, the small tin lanterns.
A thousand tambourines of crystal
wounded the light of daybreak.

Green, as I love you, greenly.
Green the wind, and green the branches.
They climbed up, the two companions.
In the mouth, the dark breezes
left there a strange flavour,
of gall, and mint, and sweet-basil.
'Brother, friend! Where is she, tell me,
where is she, your bitter beauty?
How often, she waited for you!
How often, she would have waited,
cool the face, and dark the tresses,
on this green veranda!'

Over the cistern's surface
the gypsy girl was rocking.
Green the flesh is, green the tresses,
with eyes of frozen silver.
An ice-ray made of moonlight
holding her above the water.

How intimate the night became,

like a little, hidden plaza.

Drunken Civil Guards were beating,

beating, beating on the door frame.

Green, as I love you, greenly.

Green the wind, and green the branches.

The dark ship on the sea,

and the horse on the mountain.

Note: Cabra is south-east of Córdoba, and north of Málaga, in the mountains of Andalusia. Lorca said 'If you ask me why I wrote "A thousand tambourines of crystal, wounded the light of daybreak – Mil panderos di cristal, herían la madruga" I will tell you that I saw them in the hands of trees and angels, but I cannot say more: I cannot explain their meaning. And that is how it should be. Through poetry a man more quickly reaches the cutting edge that the philosopher and the mathematician silently turn away from.'

From: Gypsy Ballads (Romancero Gitano), 1924-1927

The Gypsy Nun (*La monja gitana*)

Silence of lime and myrtle.
Mallows in slender grasses.
The nun embroiders wallflowers
on a straw-coloured cloth.
In the chandelier, fly
seven prismatic birds.
The church grunts in the distance
like a bear belly upwards.
How she sews! With what grace!
On the straw-coloured cloth
she wants to embroider
the flowers of her fantasy.
What sunflowers! What magnolias
of sequins and ribbons!
What crocuses and moons
on the cloth over the altar!
Five grapefruit sweeten
in the nearby kitchen.
The five wounds-of-Christ
cut in Almería.
Through the eyes of the nun
two horsemen gallop.
A last quiet murmur
takes off her camisole.
And gazing at clouds and hills
in the strict distance,

her heart of sugar
and verbena breaks.
Oh, what a high plain
with twenty suns above it!
What standing rivers
her fantasy sees setting!
But she goes on with her flowers,
while standing, in the breeze,
the light plays chess
high in the lattice-window.

From: Gypsy Ballads (Romancero Gitano), 1924-1927

The Unfaithful Wife (*La casada infiel*)

So, I took her to the river
thinking she was virgin,
but it seems she had a husband.
It was the night of Saint Iago,
and it almost was a duty.
The lamps went out,
the crickets lit up.
By the last street corners
I touched her sleeping breasts,
and they suddenly had opened
like the hyacinth petals.
The starch
of her slip crackled
in my ears like silk fragments
ripped apart by ten daggers.
The tree crowns
free of silver light are larger,
and a horizon, of dogs, howls
far away from the river.

Past the hawthorns,
the reeds, and the brambles,
below her dome of hair
I made a hollow in the sand.
I took off my tie.
She took off a garment.
I my belt with my revolver.
She four bodices.

Federico García Lorca

Creamy tuberoses
or shells are not as smooth as
her skin was, or, in the moonlight,
crystals shining brilliantly.

Her thighs slipped from me
like fish that are startled,
one half full of fire,
one half full of coldness.
That night I galloped
on the best of roadways,
on a mare of nacre,
without stirrups, without bridle.
As a man I cannot tell you
the things she said to me.
The light of understanding
has made me most discreet.
Smeared with sand and kisses,
I took her from the river.
The blades of the lilies
were fighting with the air.

I behaved as what I am,
as a true gypsy.
I gave her a sewing basket,
big, with straw-coloured satin.
I did not want to love her,
for though she had a husband
she said she was a virgin
when I took her to the river.

From: Gypsy Ballads (Romancero Gitano), 1924-1927

A road near Seville, Spain
John Frederick Lewis (English, 1805-1876)
Artvee

Federico García Lorca

Ballad of the Black Sorrow
(*Romance de la pena negra*)

The beaks of cockerels dig,
searching for the dawn,
when down the dark hill
comes Soledad Montoya.
Her skin of yellow copper
smells of horse and shadow.
Her breasts, like smoky anvils,
howl round-songs.
'Soledad, who do you ask for
alone, at this hour?'
'I ask for who I ask for,
say, what is it to you?
I come seeking what I seek,
my happiness and myself.'
'Soledad of my regrets,
the mare that runs away
meets the sea at last
and is swallowed by the waves.'
'Don't recall the sea to me
for black sorrow wells
in the lands of olive-trees
beneath the murmur of leaves.'
'Soledad, what sorrow you have!
What sorrow, so pitiful!
You cry lemon juice

From: Gypsy Ballads (Romancero Gitano), 1924-1927

sour from waiting, and your lips.'
'What sorrow, so great! I run
through my house like a madwoman,
my two braids trailing on the floor,
from the kitchen to the bedroom.
What sorrow! I show clothes
and flesh made of jet.
Ay, my linen shifts!
Ay, my thighs of poppy!

'Soledad: bathe your body
with the skylarks' water
and let your heart be
at peace, Soledad Montoya.'

Down below the river sings:
flight of sky and leaves.
The new light crowns itself
with pumpkin flowers.
O sorrow of the gypsies!
Sorrow, pure and always lonely.
O sorrow of the dark river-bed
and the far dawn!

Federico García Lorca

Saint Michael (*San Miguel*)

(*Granada*)

They are seen from the verandahs
on the mountain, mountain, mountain,
mules and mules' shadows
weighed down with sunflowers.

Their eyes in the shadows
are dulled by immense night.
Salt-laden dawn rustles
in the corners of the breeze.

A sky of white mules
closes its reflective eyes,
granting the quiet half-light
a heart-filled ending.
And the water turns cold
So, no-one touches it.
Water maddened and exposed
on the mountain, mountain, mountain.

Saint Michael, covered in lace,
shows his lovely thighs,
in his tower room,
encircled by lanterns.

From: Gypsy Ballads (Romancero Gitano), 1924-1927

The Archangel, domesticated,
in the twelve-o-clock gesture,
pretends to a sweet anger
of plumage and nightingales.
Saint Michael sings in the glass,
effeminate one, of three thousand nights,
fragrant with eau-de-cologne,
and far from the flowers.

The sea dances on the sands,
a poem of balconies.
The shores of the moonlight
lose reeds, gain voices.
Field-hands are coming
eating sunflower seeds,
backsides large and dark
like planets of copper.
Tall gentlemen come by
and ladies with sad deportment,
dark-haired with nostalgia
for a past of nightingales.
And the Bishop of Manila,
blind with saffron, and poor,
speaks a two-sided mass
for the women and the men.

Federico García Lorca

Saint Michael is motionless
in the bedroom of his tower,
his petticoats encrusted
with spangles and brocades.

Saint Michael, king of globes,
and odd numbers,
in the Berberesque delicacy
of cries and windowed balconies.

Alhambra, Spain (1856)
Carl Friedrich Heinrich Werner (German, 1808-1894)
Artvee

From: Gypsy Ballads (Romancero Gitano), 1924-1927

Saint Gabriel (*San Gabriel*)

(*Seville*)

1

A lovely reed-like boy,
wide shoulders, slim waist,
skin of nocturnal apple-trees,
sad mouth and large eyes,
with nerves of hot silver,
walks the empty street.
His shoes of leather
crush the dahlias of air,
in a double-rhythm beating out
quick celestial dirges.
On the margins of the sea
there's no palm-tree his equal,
no crowned emperor,
no bright wandering-star.
When his head bends down
over his breast of jasper,
the night seeks out the plains,
because it needs to kneel.
The guitars sound only
for Saint Gabriel the Archangel,
tamer of pale moths,
and enemy of willows.

'Saint Gabriel: the child cries

in his mother's womb.

Don't forget the gypsies

gifted you your costume.'

2

Royal Annunciation,
sweetly moonlit and poorly clothed
opens the door to the starlight
that comes along the street.
The Archangel Saint Gabriel
scion of the Giralda tower,
came to pay a visit,
between a lily and a smile.
In his embroidered waistcoat
hidden crickets throbbed.
The stars of the night
turned into bells.
'Saint Gabriel: Here am I
with three nails of joy.
Your jasmine radiance folds
around my flushed cheeks.'
'God save you, Annunciation.
Dark-haired girl of wonder.
You'll have a child more beautiful
than the stems of the breeze.'
'Ah, Saint Gabriel, joy of my eyes!

From: Gypsy Ballads (Romancero Gitano), 1924-1927

Little Gabriel my darling!
I dream a chair of carnations
for you to sit on.'
'God save you, Annunciation,
sweetly moonlit and poorly clothed.
Your child will have on his breast
a mole and three scars.'
'Ah, Saint Gabriel, how you shine!
Little Gabriel my darling!
In the depths of my breasts
warm milk already wells.'
God save you, Annunciation.
Mother of a hundred houses.
Your eyes shine with arid
landscapes of horsemen.'

In amazed Annunciation's
womb, the child sings.
Three bunches of green almonds
quiver in his little voice.
Now Saint Gabriel climbed
a ladder through the air.
The stars in the night
turned to immortelles.

Federico García Lorca

Romance of the Spanish Civil Guard (*Romance de la Guardia Civil española*)

The horses are black.

The horseshoes are black.

Stains of ink and wax

shine on their capes.

They have leaden skulls

so, they do not cry.

With souls of leather

they ride down the road.

Hunchbacked and nocturnal

wherever they move, they command

silences of dark rubber

and fears of fine sand.

They pass, if they wish to pass,

and hidden in their heads

is a vague astronomy

of indefinite pistols.

    O city of the gypsies!

    Banners on street-corners.

    The moon and the pumpkin

    with preserved cherries.

    O city of the gypsies!

    Who could see you and not remember?

    City of sorrow and musk,

    with towers of cinnamon.

From: Gypsy Ballads (Romancero Gitano), 1924-1927

When night came near,
night that night deepened,
the gypsies at their forges
beat out suns and arrows.
A badly wounded stallion
knocked against all the doors.
Roosters of glass were crowing
through Jerez de la Frontera.
Naked the wind turns
the corner of surprise,
in the night silver-night
night the night deepened.

The Virgin and Saint Joseph
have lost their castanets,
and search for the gypsies
to see if they can find them.
The Virgin comes draped
in the mayoress's dress,
of chocolate papers
with necklaces of almonds.
Saint Joseph swings his arms
under a cloak of silk.
Behind comes Pedro Domecq
with three sultans of Persia.
The half-moon dreamed
an ecstasy of storks.
Banners and lanterns

invaded the flat roofs.
Through the mirrors wept
ballerinas without hips.
Water and shadow, shadow and water
through Jerez de la Frontera.

    O city of the gypsies!
    Banners on street-corners.
    Quench your green lamps
    the worthies are coming.
    O city of the gypsies!
    Who could see you and not remember?
    Leave her far from the sea
    without combs in her hair.

They ride two abreast
towards the festive city.
A murmur of immortelles
invades the cartridge-belts.
They ride two abreast.
A doubled nocturne of cloth.
They fancy the sky to be
a showcase for spurs.

The city, free from fear,
multiplied its doors.
Forty civil guards
enter them to plunder.

From: Gypsy Ballads (Romancero Gitano), 1924-1927

The clocks came to a halt,
and the cognac in the bottles
disguised itself as November
so as not to raise suspicion.

A flight of intense shrieks
rose from the weathercocks.
The sabers chopped at the breezes
that the hooves trampled.
Along the streets of shadow
old gypsy women ran,
with the drowsy horses,
and the jars of coins.
Through the steep streets
sinister cloaks climb,
leaving behind them
whirlwinds of scissors.

At a gate to Bethlehem
the gypsies congregate.
Saint Joseph, wounded everywhere,
shrouds a young girl.
Stubborn rifles crack
sounding in the night.
The Virgin heals children
with spittle from a star.
But the Civil Guard
advance, sowing flames,

where young and naked
imagination is burnt out.
Rosa of the Camborios
moans in her doorway,
with her two severed breasts
lying on a tray.
And other girls ran
chased by their tresses
through air where roses
of black gunpowder burst.
When all the roofs
were furrows in the earth
the dawn heaved its shoulders
in a vast silhouette of stone.

    O city of the gypsies!
    The Civil Guards depart
    through a tunnel of silence
    while flames surround you.

    O city of the gypsies!
    Who could see you and not remember?
    Let them find you on my forehead:
    a play of moon and sand.

From: Gypsy Ballads (Romancero Gitano), 1924-1927

Sketches in Spain (1837)
David Roberts (Scottish, 1796-1864)
Artvee

Federico García Lorca

Thamar and Amnon (*Thamar y Amnón*)

The moon turns in the sky
over lands without water
while the summer sows
murmurs of tiger and flame.
Over the roofs
metal nerves jangled.
Rippling air stirred
with woolly bleating.
The earth offered itself
full of scarred wounds,
or shuddering with the fierce
searing of white light.

Thamar was dreaming
of birds in her throat
to the sound of cold tambourines
and moonlit zithers.
Her nakedness in the eaves,
the sharp north of a palm-tree,
demands snowflakes on her belly,
and hailstones on her shoulders.
Thamar was singing
naked on the terrace.
Around her feet
five frozen pigeons.
Amnon, slim, precise,

From: Gypsy Ballads (Romancero Gitano), 1924-1927

watched her from the tower,
with thighs of foam,
and quivering beard.
Her bright nakedness
was stretched out on the terrace
with the murmur in her teeth
of a newly struck arrow.
Amnon was gazing
at the low, round moon,
and, in the moon, he saw
his sister's hard breasts.

Amnon lay on his bed
at half past three.
The whole room suffered
from his eyes filled with wings.
The solid light buries
villages in brown sand,
or reveals the ephemeral
coral of roses and dahlias.
Pure captive well-water
gushes silence into jars.
The cobra stretches, sings
in the moss of tree-trunks.
Amnon moans among
the coolness of bed-sheets.
The ivy of a shiver
clothes his burning flesh.

Thamar enters silently
through the room's silence,
the colour of vein and Danube,
troubled by distant footprints.
'Thamar, erase my vision
with your certain dawn.
The threads of my blood weave
frills on your skirt.'
'Let me be, brother,
your kisses on my shoulder
are wasps and little breezes
in a double swarm of flutes.'
'Thamar, you have in your high breasts
two fishes that call to me,
and in your fingertips
the murmur of a captive rose.'

The king's hundred horses
neighed in the courtyard.
The slenderness of the vine
resisted buckets of sunlight.
Now he grasps her by the hair,
now he tears her under-garments.
Warm corals drawing streams
on a light-coloured map.

From: Gypsy Ballads (Romancero Gitano), 1924-1927

Oh, what cries were heard
above the houses!
What a thicket of knives
and torn tunics.
Slaves go up and down
the saddened stairs.
Thighs and pistons play
under stationary clouds.
Gypsy virgins scream
around Thamar,
others gather drops
from her martyred flower.
White cloths redden
in the closed rooms.
Murmurs of warm daybreak
changing vines and fishes.

Amnon, angry violator,
flees on his pony.
Dark-skinned men loose arrows at him
from the walls and towers.
And when the four hooves
become four echoes,
King David cuts his harp-strings
with a pair of scissors.

Federico García Lorca

From: Poet in New York (Poeta en Nueva York), 1929-1930

The Dawn (*La aurora*)

New York's dawn holds
four mud pillars,
and a hurricane of black doves,
paddling in foul water.

New York's dawn
moans on vast stairways,
searching on the ledges,
for anguished tuberoses.

Dawn breaks and no one's mouth breathes it,
since hope and tomorrow, here, have no meaning.
Sometimes coins, furiously swarming,
stab and devour the abandoned children.

The first to go outside know in their bones
Paradise will not be there, nor wild loves.
They know they go to the swamp of law, and numbers,
to play without art, and labour without fruit.

From: Poet in New York (Poeta en Nueva York), 1929-1930

The light is buried by chains and by noise,

in the shameless challenge, of rootless science.

All across the suburbs, sleepless crowds stumble,

as if saved, by the moment, from a shipwreck of blood.

Federico García Lorca

Double Poem of Lake Eden
(*Poema doble del lago Edén*)

'Our cattle graze, the wind breathes.'
Garcilaso

It was my ancient voice
ignorant of thick bitter juices.
I sense it lapping my feet
beneath the fragile wet ferns.

Ay, ancient voice of my love,
ay, voice of my truth,
ay, voice of my open flank,
when all the roses flowed from my tongue
and grass knew nothing of horses' impassive teeth!

Here are you drinking my blood,
drinking my tedious childhood mood,
while in the wind my eyes are bludgeoned
by aluminium and drunken voices.

Let me pass the gates
where Eve eats ants
and Adam seeds dazzled fish.
Let me return, manikins with horns,
to the grove where I stretch
and leap with joy.

From: Poet in New York (Poeta en Nueva York), 1929-1930

I know a rite so secret
it requires an old rusty pin
and I know the horror of open eyes
on a plate's concrete surface.

But I want neither world nor dream, nor divine voice,
I want my freedom, my human love
in the darkest corner of breeze that no one wants.
My human love!

Those hounds of the sea chase each other
and the wind spies on careless tree trunks.
O ancient voice, burn with your tongue
this voice of tin and talc!

I long to weep because I want to,
as the children cry in the last row,
because I'm not man, nor poet, nor leaf,
but only a wounded pulse circling the things of the other side.

I want to cry out speaking my name,
rose, child and fir-tree beside this lake,
to speak my truth as a man of blood
slay in myself the tricks and turns of the word.

No, no. I'm not asking, I, desire,
voice, my freedom that laps my hands.
In the labyrinth of screens, it's my nakedness receives
the moon of punishment and the ash-drowned clock.

Thus, I was speaking.

Thus, I was speaking when Saturn stopped the trains,

when the fog and Dream and Death were seeking me.

Seeking me

where the cows, with tiny pages' feet, bellow

and where my body floats between opposing fulcrums.

From: Poet in New York (Poeta en Nueva York), 1929-1930

Death

What effort!

What effort the horse exerts

To be a dog!

What effort the dog to become a swallow!

What effort the swallow to become a bee!

What effort the bee to become a horse!

And the horse,

what a sharp shaft it steals from the rose!

what grey rosiness lifts from its lips!

And the rose,

what a flock of lights and cries

caught in the living sap of its stem!

And the sap,

what thorns it dreams in its vigil!

And the tiny daggers

what moon, and no stable, what nakedness,

skin eternal and reddened, they go seeking!

And I, in the eaves,

what a burning seraph I seek and am!

But the arch of plaster,

how vast, invisible, how minute,

without effort!

Federico García Lorca

Ode to Walt Whitman

By the East River and the Bronx
boys sang, stripped to the waist,
along with the wheels, oil, leather and hammers.
Ninety thousand miners working silver from rock
and the children drawing stairways and perspectives.

But none of them slumbered,
none of them wished to be river,
none loved the vast leaves,
none the blue tongue of the shore.

By East River and the Queensboro
boys battled with Industry,
and Jews sold the river faun
the rose of circumcision
and the sky poured, through bridges and rooftops,
herds of bison driven by the wind.

But none would stop,
none of them longed to be cloud,
none searched for ferns
or the tambourine's yellow circuit.

When the moon sails out
pulleys will turn to trouble the sky;
a boundary of needles will fence in memory
and coffins will carry off those who don't work.

From: Poet in New York (Poeta en Nueva York), 1929-1930

New York of mud,

New York of wire and death.

What angel lies hidden in your cheek?

What perfect voice will speak the truth of wheat?

Who the terrible dream of your stained anemones?

View of South Street, from Maiden Lane, New York City (ca. 1827)
William James Bennett (English, 1787–1844)
Artvee

Not for a single moment, Walt Whitman, lovely old man,

have I ceased to see your beard filled with butterflies,

nor your corduroy shoulders frayed by the moon,

nor your thighs of virgin Apollo,

nor your voice like a column of ash;

ancient beautiful as the mist,

who moaned as a bird does
its sex pierced by a needle.
Enemy of the satyr,
enemy of the vine
and lover of the body under rough cloth.

Not for a single moment, virile beauty
who in mountains of coal, billboards, railroads,
dreamed of being a river and slumbering like a river
with that comrade who would set in your breast
the small grief of an ignorant leopard.

Not for a single moment, Adam of blood, Male,
man alone on the sea, Walt Whitman, lovely old man,
because on penthouse roofs,
and gathered together in bars,
emerging in squads from the sewers,
trembling between the legs of chauffeurs
or spinning on dance-floors of absinthe,
the *maricas*, Walt Whitman, point to you.

Him too! He's one! And they hurl themselves
at your beard luminous and chaste,
blonds from the north, blacks from the sands,
multitudes with howls and gestures,
like cats and like snakes,
the *maricas*, Walt Whitman, *maricas*,
disordered with tears, flesh for the whip,
for the boot, or the tamer's bite.

From: Poet in New York (Poeta en Nueva York), 1929-1930

Him too! He's one! Stained fingers
point to the shore of your dream,
when a friend eats your apple,
with its slight tang of petrol,
and the sun sings in the navels
of the boys at play beneath bridges.

But you never sought scratched eyes,
nor the darkest swamp where they drown the children,
nor the frozen saliva,
nor the curved wounds like a toad's belly
that *maricas* bear, in cars and on terraces,
while the moon whips them on terror's street-corners.

You sought a nakedness like a river.
Bull and dream that would join the wheel to the seaweed,
father of your agony, camellia of your death,
and moan in the flames of your hidden equator.

For it is right that a man not seek his delight
in the bloody jungle of approaching morning.
The sky has shores where life is avoided
and bodies that should not be echoed by dawn.

Agony, agony, dream, ferment and dream.
This is the world, my friend, agony, agony.
Bodies dissolve beneath city clocks,
war passes weeping with a million grey rats,

the rich give their darlings

little bright dying things,

and life is not noble, or sacred, or good.

Man can, if he wishes, lead his desire

through a vein of coral or a heavenly nude.

Tomorrow loves will be stones and Time

a breeze that comes slumbering through the branches.

That's why I don't raise my voice, old Walt Whitman,

against the boy who inscribes

the name of a girl on his pillow,

nor the lad who dresses as a bride

in the shadow of the wardrobe,

nor the solitary men in clubs

who drink with disgust prostitution's waters,

nor against the men with the green glance

who love men and burn their lips in silence.

But yes, against you, city *maricas*,

of tumescent flesh and unclean thought.

Mothers of mud. Harpies. Unsleeping enemies

of Love that bestows garlands of joy.

From: Poet in New York (Poeta en Nueva York), 1929-1930

Against you forever, you who give boys

drops of foul death with bitter poison.

Against you forever,

Fairies of North America,

Pájaros of Havana,

Jotos of Mexico,

Sarasas of Cádiz,

Apios of Seville,

Cancos of Madrid,

Floras of Alicante,

Adelaidas of Portugal.

Maricas of all the world, murderers of doves!

Slaves to women. Their boudoir bitches.

Spread in public squares like fevered fans

or ambushed in stiff landscapes of hemlock.

No quarter! Death

flows from your eyes

and heaps grey flowers at the swamp's edge.

No quarter! Look out!!

Let the perplexed, the pure,

the classical, noted, the supplicants

close the gates of the bacchanal to you.

Federico García Lorca

And you, lovely Walt Whitman, sleep on the banks of the Hudson

with your beard towards the pole and your hands open.

Bland clay or snow, your tongue is calling

for comrades to guard your disembodied gazelle.

Sleep: nothing remains.

A dance of walls stirs the prairies

and America drown itself in machines and lament.

I long for a fierce wind that from deepest night

shall blow the flowers and letters from the vault where you sleep

and a dark-skinned boy to tell the whites and their gold

that the kingdom of wheat has arrived.

From: Poet in New York (Poeta en Nueva York), 1929-1930

The Poet Arrives in Havana
(*El poeta llega a la Habana*)

When the moon's risen fully I'm off to Santiago, Cuba,
off to Santiago
in a wagon of black water.
Off to Santiago.
Singing palms above the roof-tops.
Off to Santiago.
When the palm-tree wants to be stork,
off to Santiago.
And the banana-tree jellyfish,
I'm off to Santiago.
Off to Santiago
with the blond head of Fonseca.
Off to Santiago.
With the rose, Juliet's and Romeo's,
off to Santiago.
Sea of paper, coins of silver,
off to Santiago.
Oh, Cuba! Oh, rhythm of dried seeds!
Off to Santiago.
Oh, waist of fire, drop of wood!
Off to Santiago.
Harp of living tree-trunks. Caiman. Flower of tobacco.
Off to Santiago.
I always said I'd be off, off to Santiago,
in a wagon of black water.

Off to Santiago.

Air and alcohol on the wheels,

I'm going to Santiago.

My coral in the twilight,

off to Santiago.

The ocean drowned in the sand,

off to Santiago.

Heat whitening, fruit rotting,

off to Santiago.

Oh, the sugar-cane's dumb coolness!

Oh, Cuba, curve of sigh and clay!

I'm off to Santiago.

From: *Bodas de sangre: Blood Wedding: Act I: 1933*

Lullaby of the Great Stallion
(*Nana del caballo grande*)

GRANDMOTHER:

A singing, child, a singing
> about the great stallion,
> who would not drink the water,
>> the water in its blackness,
>> in among the branches.
>> Where it finds the bridge,
>> it hangs there, singing.
>> Who knows what water is,
>> my child,
>> its tail waving,
>> through the dark green chambers?

MOTHER (softly): Sleep, my flower,
> the stallion is not drinking.

GRANDMOTHER: Sleep, my rose,
> the stallion is crying.
> His legs are wounded,
> his mane is frozen,
> in his eyes,

there is a blade of silver.
They went to the river.
Ay, how they went!
Blood running,
quicker than water.

MOTHER: Sleep, my flower,
the stallion is not drinking.

GRANDMOTHER: Sleep, my rose,
the stallion is crying.

MOTHER: It would not touch
the wet shore,
his burning muzzle,
silvered with flies.
He would only neigh,
to the harsh mountains,
a weight of river, dead,
against his throat.
Ay, proud stallion
that would not drink the water!
Ay, pain of snowfall,
stallion of daybreak!

GRANDMOTHER: Do not come here! Wait,
close the window,
with branches of dream,
and dreams of branches.

MOTHER: My child is sleeping.

GRANDMOTHER: My child is silent.

From: Bodas de sangre: Blood Wedding: Act I: 1933

MOTHER: Stallion, my child
has a soft pillow.

GRANDMOTHER: Steel for his cradle.

MOTHER: Lace for his covers.

GRANDMOTHER: A singing, child, a singing.

MOTHER: Ay, proud stallion
that would not drink the water!

GRANDMOTHER: Don't come here! Don't enter!
Go up to the mountain
through the sombre valley,
to where the wild mare is.

MOTHER (gazing): My child is sleeping.

GRANDMOTHER: My child is resting.

MOTHER (softly): Sleep, my flower,
the stallion is not drinking.

GRANDMOTHER (rising, and very softly):

Sleep, my rose,
the stallion is crying.

Federico García Lorca

From: Llanto por Ignacio Sánchez Mejías, 1935

Lament for Ignacio Sánchez Mejías

The Goring and the Death

At five in the afternoon.
It was just five in the afternoon.
A boy brought the white sheet
at five in the afternoon.
A basket of lime made ready
at five in the afternoon.
The rest was death and only death
at five in the afternoon.

The wind blew the cotton wool away
at five in the afternoon.
And oxide scattered nickel and glass
at five in the afternoon.
Now the dove and the leopard fight
at five in the afternoon.
And a thigh with a desolate horn
at five in the afternoon.
The bass-pipe sound began
at five in the afternoon.
The bells of arsenic, the smoke

From: Llanto por Ignacio Sánchez Mejías, 1935

at five in the afternoon.
Silent crowds on corners
at five in the afternoon.
And only the bull with risen heart!
at five in the afternoon.
When the snow-sweat appeared
at five in the afternoon.
when the arena was splashed with iodine
at five in the afternoon.
death laid its eggs in the wound
at five in the afternoon.
At five in the afternoon.
At just five in the afternoon.

A coffin on wheels for his bed
at five in the afternoon.
Bones and flutes sound in his ear
at five in the afternoon.
Now the bull bellows on his brow
at five in the afternoon.
The room glows with agony
at five in the afternoon.
Now out of distance gangrene comes
at five in the afternoon.
Trumpets of lilies for the green groin
at five in the afternoon.
Wounds burning like suns
at five in the afternoon,

Street Scene in Granada on the Day of the Bullfight (1833)
John Frederick Lewis (English, 1805-1876)
Yale Center for British Art

From: Llanto por Ignacio Sánchez Mejías, 1935

and the people smashing windows
at five in the afternoon.
At five in the afternoon.
Ay, what a fearful five in the afternoon!
It was five on every clock!
It was five of a dark afternoon!

The Spilt Blood

I don't want to see it!

Tell the moon to come,
I don't want to see the blood
of Ignacio on the sand.

I don't want to see it!

The moon wide open,
mare of still clouds,
and the grey bullring of dream
with osiers in the barriers.

I don't want to see it!
How the memory burns me.
Inform the jasmines
with their tiny whiteness!

I don't want to see it!

The heifer of the ancient world
licked her saddened tongue
over a snout-full of blood
spilled on the sand,
and the bulls of Guisando,
part death, and part stone,
bellowed like two centuries
weary of pawing the ground.
No.
I don't want to see it!

Ignacio climbs the tiers
with all his death on his shoulders.
He was seeking the dawn,
and the dawn was not there.
He seeks his perfect profile
and sleep disorients him.
He was seeking his lovely body
and met his gushing blood.
Don't ask me to look!
I don't want to feel the flow
any more, its ebbing force:
the flow that illuminates
the front rows and spills
over the leather and corduroy
of the thirsty masses.
Who calls me to appear?
Don't ask me to look!

From: Llanto por Ignacio Sánchez Mejías, 1935

His eyes did not shut
when he saw the horns nearby,
though the terrifying mothers
lifted up their heads.
And sweeping the herds
came a breeze of secret voices,
ranchers of the pale mist, calling
to the bulls of the sky.

There was never a prince of Seville
to compare with him,
nor a sword like his sword,
nor a heart so true.
His marvellous strength
like a river of lions
and like a marble torso
the profile of his judgment.
The air of an Andalusian Roma
gilded his head,
while his laughter was a tuberose
of wit and intellect.
How great a bullfighter in the arena!
How fine a mountaineer in the sierra!
How gentle with ears of wheat!
How fierce with the spurs!
How tender with the dew!
How dazzling at the fair!
How tremendous with the last
banderillas of darkness!

But now his sleep is endless.
Now the mosses and grass
open with skilled fingers
the flower of his skull.
And now his blood goes singing:
singing through marsh and meadows,
sliding down numbed horns,
wandering soulless in mist
encountering a thousand hooves
like a long dark tongue of sadness
to form a pool of agony
near the starry Guadalquivir.

O white wall of Spain!
O black bull of sorrow!
O hardened blood of Ignacio!
O nightingale of his veins!

No.
I don't want to see it!
There's no cup to hold it,
no swallow to drink it,
no frost of light to cool it,
no song, no deluge of lilies,
no crystal to silver it.
No.
I don't want to see it!!

From: Llanto por Ignacio Sánchez Mejías, 1935

The Body Laid-Out

The stone is a brow where dreams groan,
holding no winding water or frozen cypress.
The stone is a shoulder to bear time
with trees of tears, ribbons, planets.

I have watched grey rains running to the waves
lifting their fragile, riddled arms,
so as not to be caught by the outstretched stone
that unties their limbs without drinking their blood.

Because stone collects seeds and banks of cloud,
skeletons of larks and twilight wolves,
but gives up no sounds, crystals, fire, only bullrings
and bullrings, and more bullrings with no walls.

Now Ignacio the well-born lies on the stone.
Now it's done. What passes? Contemplate his form!
Death has covered him with pale sulphur
given him the head of a dark minotaur.

Now it's done! Rain penetrates his mouth.
Air rises mad from his sunken chest,
and love, soaked with tears of snow,
warms himself on the heights among herds.

Federico García Lorca

What are they saying? A stinking silence settles.
We are with a laid-out corpse that vanishes,
with a clear form that held nightingales
and we see it riddled with countless holes.

Who disturbs the shroud? It's not true what he says!
No one's singing here, or weeps in a corner,
or pricks his spurs, or frightens off snakes:
here I want nothing but open eyes
to see that body that can't rest.

I want to see the men with harsh voices here.
Those who tame horses and subdue rivers:
the men who rattle their bones and sing
with a mouth full of sun and flints.

I want to see them here. In front of the stone.
In front of this body with broken sinews.
I want them to show me where there's an exit
for this captain bound by death.

I want them to show me grief like a river
that has sweet mists and steep banks
to bear Ignacio's body, and let him be lost
without hearing the double snort of the bulls.

Let him be lost in the moon's round bullring
that imitates, new, a bull stilled by pain.
let him be lost in the night with no singing of fish
and in the white weeds of congealed smoke.

From: Llanto por Ignacio Sánchez Mejías, 1935

I don't want them to cover his face with a cloth,
so, he can grow accustomed to death that he bears.
Go, Ignacio: don't feel the hot bellowing.
Sleep, soar, rest: even the ocean dies!

The Soul Absent

Neither the bull nor the fig tree knows you,
nor your horses, nor the ants under your floor.
Neither the child nor the evening knows you,
because you have died forever.

The spine of rock does not know you,
nor the black satin where you are ruined,
Your mute remembrance does not know you,
because you have died forever.

Autumn will come with its snails,
grapes in mist, and clustered mountains,
but no one will want to gaze in your eyes,
because you have died forever.

Because you have died forever,
like all the dead of the Earth,
like all the dead forgotten
in a pile of lifeless curs.

Federico García Lorca

No one knows you. No. But I sing of you.
I sing for others your profile and grace.
The famed ripeness of your understanding.
Your appetite for death, pleasure in its savour.
The sadness your valiant gaiety contained.

Not for a long time, if ever, will there be born,
an Andalusian so brilliant, so rich in adventure.
I sing his elegance in words that moan,
and remember a sad breeze through the olive-trees.

Interior Of The Cathedral Of Ávila (Spain)
Heinrich Hermanns (German, 1862 - 1942)
Artvee

From: Six Galician Poems (Seis poemas Gallegos), 1935

Madrigal for the City of Santiago

It rains on Santiago
my sweet love.
White camellia of air,
sunlight in a veil.

It rains on Santiago,
in the dark night.
Grass of silver and dream
covers the empty moon.

See the rain in the streets,
the lament of stone and glass.
See on the fading wind
your sea's shadow and ash.

Your sea's shadow and ash,
Santiago, far from the sun:
shivering in my heart,
water of ancient dawn.

Federico García Lorca

Nocturne of the Drowned Youth

Let's go, silent, down by the ford
to see the youth drowned in the water.

Let's go, silent, to the banks of air,
before the stream takes him down to the sea.

His soul wept, tiny and wounded,
under pine-needles and grasses.

Water fell, hurled by the moon,
clothed the naked mountain with violets.

The wind threw camellias of twilight
into the parched light of his sad mouth.

Come, blind boys of mountain and field,
come see the youth who drowned in the water.

Come shadowy folk of the valleys and peaks,
before the stream takes him down to the sea.

It carries him down to the sea's white curtain
where old oxen come and go in the water.

Ay, how the trees by the river sang
over the green moon's tambourine!

Boys, let's go, now, hurry, away!
Because the stream takes him down to the sea!

From: Six Galician Poems (Seis poemas Gallegos), 1935

Dance of the Santiago Moon

Look at that white gallant
look at his wasted flesh!

It's the moon that's dancing
in the Courtyard of the Dead.

Look at his wasted flesh,
black with twilight and wolves.

Mother: The moon dances
in the Courtyard of the Dead.

Who wounds the horse of stone
at the gates of sleep?

It's the moon! It's the moon
in the Courtyard of the Dead!

Who looks in my grey windows,
with an eye full of cloud?

It's the moon! It's the moon
in the Courtyard of the Dead!

Let me die in my bed
dreaming the flower of gold.

Federico García Lorca

Mother: The moon dances
in the Courtyard of the Dead.

Ay, daughter, the air in the sky
has suddenly turned me white!

It isn't the air, it's the sad moon
in the Courtyard of the Dead.

Who groans with that groan
of an ox, huge and malcontent?

Mother: It's the moon, the moon
in the Courtyard of the Dead.

Yes, the moon, the moon,
crowned with yellow gorse,
that dances, dances, dances,
in the Courtyard of the Dead!

From: The Tamarit Divan (Diván del Tamarit), 1936

Ghazal of Unexpected Love
(*Gacela del amor imprevisto*)

No one understood the perfume
of the shadow magnolia of your belly.
No one knew you crushed completely
a humming-bird of love between your teeth.

There slept a thousand little Persian horses
in the moonlight plaza of your forehead,
while, for four nights, I embraced there
your waist, the enemy of snowfall.

Between the plaster and the jasmines,
your gaze was a pale branch, seeding.
I tried to give you, in my breastbone,
the ivory letters that say *ever*.

Ever, ever: garden of my torture,
your body, flies from me forever,
the blood of your veins is in my mouth now,
already light-free for my death.

Federico García Lorca

Ghazal of the Terrible Presence
(*Gacela de la terrible presencia*)

I want the river to lose its way.
I want the wind to quit the valley.

I want the night to lose its sight,
and my heart its flower of gold;

the cattle to speak to the great leaves,
and the worm to die of shadows;

the teeth on the skull to shine,
and the silk to be drowned in yellows.

I can see wounded midnight's duel
struggling, knotted, with noon light.

I resist the broken arch, where time suffers,
and the green venom of twilight.

But do not make a black cactus,
open in reeds, of your nakedness.

Leave me afraid of dark planets,
but do not show me your calm waist.

From: The Tamarit Divan (Diván del Tamarit), 1936

Ghazal of the Bitter Root
(*Gacela de la raíz amarga*)

There's a bitter root
and a world of a thousand terraces.
Not even the smallest hand
shatters the gate of waters.

Where are you going, where, where?
There's a sky of a thousand windows
– a battle of bruised bees –
and there's a bitter root.

Bitter.

Sore on the sole of the foot,
on the inside of the face,
and sore in the cool trunk
of the freshly cut night.

Love, my enemy,
bite on your bitter root!

Federico García Lorca

Ghazal of the Flight
(*Gacela de la huida*)

Often, I lost myself in the sea,
my ears filled with fresh-cut flowers
my tongue filled with love and anguish.
Often, I lost myself in the sea,
as I am lost in the hearts of children.

No one when giving a kiss
fails to feel the smile of faceless people.
No one who touches a new-born child,
forgets the immobile skulls of horses.

Because the roses search the forehead,
for the toughened landscapes of bone,
and Man's hands have no fate,
but to imitate roots, under the ground.

As I am lost in the hearts of children,
often, I lost myself in the sea.
Ignorant of water, I go searching,
for death, in light, consuming me.

From: The Tamarit Divan (Diván del Tamarit), 1936

Ghazal of Dark Death
(*Gacela de la muerte oscura*)

I want to sleep the sleep of apples,
far from the tumult of cemeteries.
I want to sleep the sleep of that child
who longed to cut out his heart at sea.

I don't wish to hear that the dead lose no blood;
that the shattered mouth still begs for water.
don't wish to know of torments granted by grass,
nor of the moon with the serpent's mouth
that goes to work before dawn.

I want to sleep for a while,
a while, a minute, a century;
as long as all know I am not dead;
that in my lips is a golden manger;
that I'm the slight friend of the West Wind;
that I'm the immense shadow of tears.

Cover me, at dawn, with a veil
since she'll hurl at me fistfuls of ants;
and wet my shoes with harsh water
so, her scorpion's sting will slide by.

For I want to sleep the sleep of apples
learn a lament that will cleanse me of earth;
for I want to live with that hidden child
who longed to cut out his heart at sea.

Federico García Lorca

Casida of One Wounded by Water
(*Casida del herido por el agua*)

I want to descend the well,
I want to climb the walls of Granada,
To gaze at the heart graved
By the dark stylus of waters.

The wounded child moaned
With a crown of frost.
Ponds, cisterns and fountains
Raised their swords in the air.
Ay! What fury of love, what a wounding edge,
what nocturnal murmurs, what white deaths!
What deserts of light went destroying
the sand-dunes of dawn!
The child was alone
With the sleeping town in his throat.
A fountain that rises from dream
guarded him from thirsts of seaweed.
The child and his agony face to face,
Were two green entangled showers.
The child stretched on the ground
his agony bent on itself.

I want to descend the well,
I want to die my death by mouthfuls,
I want to fill my heart with moss,
To see the one wounded by water.

From: The Tamarit Divan (Diván del Tamarit), 1936

View from the Alhambra, Spain (circa 1882)
William Stanley Haseltine (American, 1835-1900)
Artvee

Federico García Lorca

Casida of the Weeping (*Casida del llanto*)

I've closed my balcony;
I don't want to hear the weeping,
yet out beyond the grey walls
nothing's heard but weeping.

There are very few angels singing,
there are very few dogs barking,
a thousand violins fit in the palm of my hand.

But the weeping's a dog, immense,
the weeping's an angel, immense,
the weeping's a violin, immense
the tears have silenced the wind,
and nothing is heard but weeping.

From: The Tamarit Divan (Diván del Tamarit), 1936

Casida of the Branches (*Casida de los ramos*)

Through the trees of Tamarit
have come the hounds of lead
waiting for the branches to fall,
waiting till they shatter themselves.

Tamarit has an apple tree
with an apple on it that sobs.
A nightingale gathers the sighs
and a pheasant leads them off through the dust.

But the branches are happiness,
the branches are like us.
They don't think of rain, they sleep,
as if they were trees, just like that.

Sitting, their knees in water,
two valleys awaited the Fall.
The twilight with elephantine step
leant against trunks and branches.

Through the trees of Tamarit
are many children with veiled faces
waiting for my branches to fall,
waiting till they shatter themselves.

Federico García Lorca

Casida of the Recumbent Woman
(*Casida de la mujer tendida*)

To see you naked is to know the Earth.
The Earth glistening, empty of horses.
The Earth, reed-less, pure in form,
closed to futures, horizon of silver.

To see you naked is to see the concern
of rain searching for a fragile waist,
or the feverish sea's immense face,
not finding its own brightness.

Blood will cry in the alcoves,
enter with swords on fire,
but you will not know the cache,
of the toad's heart or the violet.

Your belly is a knot of roots,
your lips a dawn with no outline.
Under the bed's cool roses,
the dead moan, waiting their turn.

From: The Tamarit Divan (Diván del Tamarit), 1936

Casida of the Impossible Hand
(*Casida de la mano imposible*)

I want no more than a hand,
A wounded hand, if possible.
I want no more than a hand,
even if I spend a thousand nights with no bed.

It would be a pale lily of lime,
a dove it would be, chained to my heart,
the guard it would be, who on my last night
would deny the moon entrance wholly.

I want no more than that hand
for daily unction, the white sheet of my dying.
I want no more than that hand
to bear a wing of my death.

All the rest passes.
Blush now without a name. Perpetual star.
The rest is the other; sad breeze,
While the hosts of leaves flee.

Federico García Lorca

Casida of the Rose (*Casida de la Rosa*)

The rose was

not looking for the morning:

on its branch, almost immortal,

it looked for something other.

The rose was

not looking for wisdom, or for shadow:

the edge of flesh and dreaming,

it looked for something other.

The rose was

not looking for the rose, was

unmoving in the heavens:

it looked for something other.

From: The Tamarit Divan (Diván del Tamarit), 1936

Casida of the Golden Girl
(*Casida de la muchacha dorada*)

The golden girl
bathed in the water,
and the water turned gold.

The weeds and branches
in shadow surprised her,
and the nightingale sang
for the white girl.

And the bright night came,
clouded dark silver,
with barren mountains
beneath the umber breeze.

The wet girl
was white in the water
and the water, blushed.

The dawn came without stain,
with its cattle's thousand faces,
stiff and shrouded there
with frosty garlands.

The girl of tears
bathed among tears,
and the nightingale wept

with burning wings.
The golden girl
was a white heron
and the water turned her to gold.

From: The Tamarit Divan (Diván del Tamarit), 1936

Casida of the Dark Doves
(*Casida de las palomas oscuras*)

Through the laurel branches
I saw two doves of darkness.
The one it was the sun,
the other one was lunar.
I said: 'Little neighbours
where is my tombstone?'
'In my tail-feathers,' the sun said.
'In my throat,' said the lunar.
And I who was out walking
with the earth wrapped round me,
saw two eagles made of white snow,
and a girl who was naked.
And the one was the other,
and the girl, she was neither.
I said: 'Little eagles,
where is my tombstone?'
'In my tail-feathers,' the sun said.
'In my throat,' said the lunar.
Through the branches of laurel,
I saw two doves, both naked.
And the one was the other,
and the two of them were neither.

Federico García Lorca

From: Sonnets of Dark Love (Sonetos del amor oscuro), 1936

Wounds of Love (*Llagas de amor*)

This light, this flame that devours,
this grey country that surrounds me,
this pain from a sole idea,
this anguish of the sky, earth and hour,

this lament of blood that now adorns
a lyre with no pulse, lubricious torch,
this weight of sea that breaks on me,
this scorpion that lives inside my breast,

are a garland of love, bed of the wounded,
where dreamlessly, I dream of your presence
among the ruins of my sunken breast.

And though I seek the summit of discretion
your heart grants me a valley stretched below,
with hemlock and bitter wisdom's passion.

From: Sonnets of Dark Love (Sonetos del amor oscuro), 1936

Sonnet of the Wreath of Roses
(*Soneto de la guirnalda de las rosas*)

The wreath, quick, I am dying!
Weave it quick now! Sing, and moan, sing!
Now the shadow is darkening my throat,
and January's light returns, a thousand and one times.

Between what needs me, and my needing you,
starry air, and a trembling tree.
A thickness of windflowers lifts
a whole year, with hidden groaning.

Take joy from the fresh landscape of my wound,
break out the reeds, and the delicate streams,
and taste the blood, spilt, on thighs of sweetness.

But quick! So that joined together, and one,
time will find us ruined,
with bitten souls, and mouths bruised with love.

Federico García Lorca

The Poet asks his Love to write
(*El poeta pide a su amor que le escribe*)

Visceral love, living death,

in vain, I wait your written word,

and consider, with the flower that withers,

I wish to lose you, if I have to live without self.

The air is undying: the inert rock

neither knows shadow, nor evades it.

And the heart, inside, has no use

for the honeyed frost the moon pours.

But I endured you: ripped open my veins,

a tiger, a dove, over your waist,

in a duel of teeth and lilies.

So, fill my madness with speech,

or let me live in my calm

night of the soul, darkened for ever.

From: Sonnets of Dark Love (Sonetos del amor oscuro), 1936

O Secret Voice of Hidden Love!
(*Ay voz secreta del amor oscuro!*)

O secret voice of hidden love!
O bleating without wool! O wound!
O dry camellia, bitter needle!
O sea-less current, wall-less city!

O night immense with sharpened profile,
heavenly mountain, narrow valley!
O dog inside the heart, voice going,
endless silence, full-blown iris!

Let me be, hot voice of icebergs,
and do not ask me to vanish
in weeds, where sky and flesh are fruitless.

Leave my hard ivory skull forever,
have pity on me. Stop the torture!
O I am love! O I am nature!

Federico García Lorca

Sonnet of the Sweet Complaint
(*Soneto de la dulce queja*)

I'm afraid of losing the wonder
of your eyes like a statue's, or the stress
placed on my cheek at night.
by the solitary rose of your breath.

I'm afraid of being on this shore
a branch-less trunk: this deepest feeling
of having no bloom, or pulp, or clay
for the worm of my suffering.

If you're my hidden treasure,
if you're my cross, and my moist pain,
if I'm a dog, of yours, my master,

never let me lose what I have gained,
and decorate the branches of your stream
with the leaves of my enraptured autumn.

From: Sonnets of Dark Love (Sonetos del amor oscuro), 1936

Night of Insomniac Love

Night approached us, with a full moon.
I began to cry, and you to laugh.
Your contempt was a god, and my whining
a chain of doves and minutes.

Night left us. Crystal of pain
you wept for distant depths.
My sadness was a cluster of agonies,
over your fragile heart of sand.

Morning joined us on the bed,
our mouths placed over the frozen jet
of a blood, without end, that was shed.

And the sun shone through the closed balcony,
and the coral of life opened its branch,
over my shrouded heart.

Federico García Lorca

The Beloved Sleeps on the Breast of the Poet
(*El amor duerme en el pecho de poeta*)

You will never know how much I love you
because you sleep and have slept in me.
I hide you weeping, pursued
by a voice of penetrating steel.

A law that disturbs both flesh and star
pierces my aching breast now,
and clouded words have eaten at
the wings of your severe spirit.

A knot of people leaps in the gardens
waiting for your body and my pain
on horses of light with emerald manes.

But, my beloved, keep on sleeping.
Hear my shattered blood in the violins!
Beware lest they still lie in wait for us!

From: Sonnets of Dark Love (Sonetos del amor oscuro), 1936

Courting Spanish Style (1883)
José García Ramos (Spanish, 1852-1912)
Artvee

Index of First Lines

Wind of the South. 9
The afternoon speaks: 'I am thirsty for shadows!' 12
My heart rests, by the cold fountain. 14
Singing of children 16
The sea 21
Just your hot heart, ... 23
Over the horizon, lost in confusion, ... 24
The Guadalquivir's stream 28
The field 31
It begins, the lament 32
Through black butterflies 34
From the cellar issue 35
Virgin in a crinoline, ... 36
A hundred riders in mourning, ... 37
Under the orange-tree 38
A calvary, ... 39
Juan Breva had 40
Lamps of crystal 41
Death 42
The remanso of air 43
The night is coming 44
Through the indecisive 45
At the dawn of day 46
The sea has no oranges, ... 48
Córdoba. 50
Ay, the pain it costs me 51
Sapling, sapling, ... 52
Prince, ... 54
The young girl dead 55
When the moon sails out 56

Index of First Lines

The Moon is dying, dying: 57
The moon lays a long horn, ...59
The fennel, a serpent, and rushes..59
Lucía Martínez...60
If I should die, ...61
In the green morning 62
The poplar groves are going, ...63
Woodcutter. 64
By the river banks 65
A long ghost of silver moving 66
Every song..67
We travel..68
Sleep..69
A rose in the high garden that you desire............................70
From Cádiz to Gibraltar...75
That which travels 77
Turn, ...78
I want to return to childhood..79
She passes by, my girl...80
Like concentric ripples 81
Never born, never!..82
The Moon-widow 84
Seven hearts...86
On the wide sand-dune 87
Flower of sunlight..88
The law of the past encountered 90
I know that my outline will be tranquil................................91
The moon comes to the forge, ...92
Preciosa comes playing 95
In mid-ravine 98
Green, as I love you, greenly..100
Silence of lime and myrtle..104
So, I took her to the river...106
The beaks of cockerels dig, ...109
They are seen from the verandahs 111

A lovely reed-like boy,	114
The horses are black.	117
The moon turns in the sky	123
New York's dawn holds	127
It was my ancient voice.	129
What effort!	132
By the East River and the Bronx	133
When the moon's risen fully I'm off to Santiago, Cuba,	140
A singing, child, a singing	142
At five in the afternoon.	145
It rains on Santiago	156
Let's go, silent, down by the ford	157
Look at that white gallant.	158
No one understood the perfume.	160
I want the river to lose its way.	161
There's a bitter root	162
Often, I lost myself in the sea,	163
I want to sleep the sleep of apples,	164
I want to descend the well,	165
I've closed my balcony;	167
Through the trees of Tamarit	168
To see you naked is to know the Earth.	169
I want no more than a hand,	170
The rose was	171
The golden girl.	172
Through the laurel branches	174
This light, this flame that devours,	175
The wreath, quick, I am dying!	176
Visceral love, living death,	177
O secret voice of hidden love!	178
I'm afraid of losing the wonder	179
Night approached us, with a full moon.	180
You will never know how much I love you	181

About the Translator

Anthony Kline lives in England. He graduated in Mathematics from the University of Manchester, and was Chief Information Officer (Systems Director) of a large UK Company, before dedicating himself to his literary work and interests. He was born in 1947. His work consists of translations of poetry; critical works, biographical history with poetry as a central theme; and his own original poetry. He has translated into English from Latin, Ancient Greek, Classical Chinese and the European languages. He also maintains a deep interest in developments in Mathematics and the Sciences.

He continues to write predominantly for the Internet, making all works available in download format, with an added focus on the rapidly developing area of electronic books. His most extensive works are complete translations of Ovid's Metamorphoses and Dante's Divine Comedy.

Printed in Great Britain
by Amazon